to

Disabilities

ISSUES
(formerly Issues for the Nineties)

Volume 17

Editor

Craig Donnellan

Independence
Educational Publishers
Cambridge

First published by Independence
PO Box 295
Cambridge CB1 3XP
England

© Craig Donnellan 1998

Copyright

Photocopy licence

British Library Cataloguing in Publication Data
Disabilities – (Issues Series)
I. Donnellan, Craig II. Series
362.4

ISBN 1 86168 066 X

Printed in Great Britain
City Print Ltd
Milton Keynes

Typeset by
Claire Boyd

Cover
The illustration on the front cover is by
The Attic Publishing Co.

CONTENTS

Chapter One: Living With Disabilities

Chapter Two: Disabilities and Learning

Introduction

Disabilities is the seventeenth volume in the series: **Issues**. The aim of this series is to offer up-to-date information about important issues in our world.

Disabilities looks at the challenges confronting people with disabilities.

The information comes from a wide variety of sources and includes:
Government reports and statistics
Newspaper reports and features
Magazine articles and surveys
Literature from lobby groups
and charitable organisations.

It is hoped that, as you read about the many aspects of the issues explored in this book, you will critically evaluate the information presented. It is important that you decide whether you are being presented with facts or opinions. Does the writer give a biased or an unbiased report? If an opinion is being expressed, do you agree with the writer?

Disabilities offers a useful starting-point for those who need convenient access to information about the many issues involved. However, it is only a starting-point. At the back of the book is a list of organisations which you may want to contact for further information.

*****

Prejudice is the worst handicap

According to a survey, one-third of us think wheelchair users are stupid. And not only are they stupid, they complain too much – more than one in five say that the disabled should be seen and not heard, because they already have equal rights and have no cause to command any special attention. The same proportion feel awkward in the presence of a disabled person – as if disability is somehow infectious.

Liberal opinion is no doubt shocked at this level of prejudice. There are some eight million registered disabled, a huge figure even allowing for some false benefit claimants. Since this is almost one in seven of the population, one might assume that we mix pretty regularly. Yet over half of the 1,000 people questioned in the survey say that they have no regular contact with anyone disabled – a figure that rises to 60 per cent among under-35s. Prejudice is born of ignorance. With so much ignorance about the lives of the disabled, it is little wonder that the response is thus.

Our attitude to the disabled is a bizarre mixture of admiration and contempt. We all admire those plucky disabled marathon runners. The disabled Olympics is watched with an awed fascination. And yet, according to the survey, more than 40 per cent of us think that it is 'virtually impossible' for the disabled to get a job, and a third say that they should not expect to be able to use public transport. Perhaps this is why one of the disabled people who took part in a companion survey said he wanted to shout out, 'I am alive, don't ignore me.'

These findings help to explain why the debate on disability benefits has been so unsatisfactory. The scale of the disability benefit bill – £23.5bn a year – and our confused attitude means that allegations of widespread fraud are accepted almost without question. It is perfectly proper to review the process and ensure that the money is being spent appropriately. Indeed, it is curious that the level of claimants rises so steeply in unemployment blackspots. Only last week, however, a committee set up with the intention of proving fraud could find very little significant evidence.

Our attitude to the disabled is a bizarre mixture of admiration and contempt

---

But this is about more than how we allocate money. It is about prejudice. Most prejudices break down when reality hits home. The

reality is that many things the able-bodied take for granted – public transport, access to cinemas and theatres, air travel and shopping – are at best an obstacle course and at worst well-nigh impossible. So long as our attitudes remain at the level shown in the survey things are unlikely to change.

Long-term approaches are more likely to bear fruit. Groups such as Scope and the representatives of Down's Syndrome children have long argued that sending children with special needs to their own schools, although done with the best of motives, can be deeply demoralising, reinforcing the idea that they are different. They have a point. What we learn in childhood stays with us, and if we learn that the disabled cannot cope with a normal school then it is no surprise that we think they cannot cope with a normal life.

But it is not special schools as such that are the problem. Rather, as the parents who protested at Downing Street yesterday argued, it is the rigid, bureaucratic application of individual local education authorities' policies – some favour special schools, some do not – that causes heartache. There are no pat solutions. Every child is different, and should be treated as such.

The more extreme disability rights campaigners use words like 'apartheid' to describe their situation. One's first response is to bridle at the exaggeration. But the attitudes revealed in this survey show that it is nearer to truth than fiction. If the idea of community is to be more than a mere slogan, we need to begin by addressing our own prejudices, and debate how we can make the disabled full participants.

© *The Independent*
May, 1998

Disability daily

Exploding the myths

Introduction

There are many myths and misconceptions surrounding disability and disabled people, for example:

'Disabled people are always sick, aren't they?'

'They constantly need help and are dependent on others.'

Or perhaps you think disabled people are brave and courageous; overcoming personal tragedy in the face of so much adversity, they should be admired . . .

If you think that any of these statements may be true, or if you are not sure, this article will set the record straight. It is an attempt to collect the most common myths about disabled people and their lives and spell out the true facts as we see them.

Education and Employment

As for anyone, education and employment are cornerstones to disabled people's lives. There are many myths surrounding the capabilities of disabled people in this area. Here are some of the most common.

'Disabled people are always sick and therefore unemployable.'

False . . . A survey by Barclays Bank of its staff showed that, on average, disabled staff had 8 days absence due to sickness over a two-year period, whereas non-disabled staff had an average of 10 days.[1]

'The reason why so few disabled people have jobs is that they don't want to or are unable to work.'

False . . . Disabled people do want to work. Unfortunately, employers often just assume that disabled people are not capable. Some disabled people can only work reduced hours but cannot manage on a part-time wage. Flexibility from employers, plus a change in the benefit rules to make it easier for people to try out employment, could assist many disabled people into work.

'People with learning difficulties can't learn.'

False . . . Just because people with learning disabilities learn at a slower rate than others it does not mean that they cannot learn.

'Disabled children are better off in special schools.'

False . . . With proper support, an integrated education can be an enriching experience for both disabled and non-disabled children.

Transport

Transport is the key to independence! Transport enables people to participate – seek and find that job, join that class or club and go shopping. But for disabled people, lack of accessible transport means exclusion and isolation from the day-to-day activities that non-disabled people take for granted.

'The new Disability Discrimination Act will make all transport accessible.'

False . . . The Disability Discrimination Act has made provision for guidelines on transport standards. These will be phased in over 20 years

and still leave airlines, ferries and all existing vehicles over 20 years old untouched.

'Making transport accessible to disabled people is expensive and a waste of resources.'

False . . . Cost is incurred, but this should be seen as an investment, as accessible transport means accessible to all. Parents with young children/buggies, people with suitcases, shopping, elderly and disabled people, will all benefit from a fully accessible integrated transport system.

Communication

Life is all about communication. Good communication leads to better understanding.

'If you use a hearing aid you can hear everything.'

False . . . Hearing aids pick up background noise and can be uncomfortable for the user. Sometimes hearing aids only help people pick up selective words, so it helps if you look at the person when speaking to them, speaking clearly and at a reasonable speed.

'All deaf people use sign language.'

False . . . Only 50,000 in the UK use sign language, although for these people, communicating in sign language may be essential, as it is their first language.[2]

'All blind people read Braille.'

False . . . Of the one million registrable blind and partially sighted people, only 19,000 read Braille. However, for these people Braille is essential.[3] Some visually impaired people prefer documents on audio cassette. Others require information in large print.

'Deafblind people have a "super" sense of smell and touch.'

False . . . A deafblind person may use their other senses to a greater extent but these senses do not develop miraculously to compensate.

'People who can't speak clearly are not intelligent.'
False . . . A speech or language impairment does not affect a person's intellectual capacity.

Living in the community

Independent living, in our society, is what people aspire to. Many people do not believe disabled people have these aspirations nor that this would be a possible life choice for them.

'Severely disabled people are best looked after in a home and cannot lead an independent life.'
False . . . Severely disabled people can lead a full and active life. Many of the problems they face are not related to their impairment but a lack of services suitable to their needs.

'We cannot sleep safely in our beds, our children are at risk from people with mental health problems.'
False . . . A diagnosis of mental illness is not in itself a predictor of violence. Despite this, two-thirds of all media references to mental illness focused on violence.[4]

'It is too expensive to build accessible houses.'
False . . . According to research, the additional cost for building a new accessible three-bedroom house, is between £100 and £350.[5]

Carers

There are nearly 7 million people throughout the UK who have some form of caring responsibility. These carers provide care and support worth an estimated £30 billion a year.[6]

'Carers are middle-aged women who wouldn't be working anyway.'
False . . . Carers can be as young as seven or as old as 97. 2.9 million carers are men. 15 per cent of carers also work. Many carers are disabled themselves. Thousands of carers provide support for over 100 hours per week.[7]

'There is adequate financial compensation for carers.'
False . . . Help for some carers is provided but is totally inadequate. Carers under 65 years old who spend at least 35 hours a week caring for a severely disabled person might get Invalid Care Allowance. However, the weekly rate of this benefit is only £37.35.

Social Security

Social Security – a crucial issue for disabled people as three out of four rely on social security benefits as their main source of income. What are the myths surrounding benefits?

'Disability benefits? . . . They are relatively generous.'
False . . . For example, long-term Incapacity Benefit, payable to people who cannot work because of disability or long-term sickness, is worth £3,247 a year. This is approximately 18% of average male earnings.[8]

'Almost anyone can get a disability benefit; you don't have to be really disabled.'
False . . . All disability benefits have strict eligibility criteria and need independent verification from a doctor or similar professional. The DSS can require any claimant to attend a full medical examination. The experience of advice agencies is that many disabled people fail to claim the benefits they are entitled to.

'People shouldn't be claiming disability benefits and working.'
False . . . It is perfectly legitimate for someone who gets Disability Living Allowance (DLA) to go out to work. DLA is not means-tested and is designed to help people with the extra costs of disability. In fact, some people are only able to retain a job because their DLA mobility component helps with their extra transport costs.

General myths

There is a whole range of other myths about disabled people and their capabilities. Here are some of them.

'It's easier being disabled if you were born that way, because then you don't know anything different.'
False . . . Being disabled is often made difficult for people because of the way other people react to impairment, and because of the lack of facilities available for disabled people. This can apply to all disabled people – whether they are born disabled or whether they acquire their disability.

'Arthritis is just wear and tear in the joints and is part and parcel of getting old.'
False . . . Arthritis is not caused by wear and tear in the joints. There are over 200 different forms of arthritis. Arthritis affects the connective tissues surrounding the joint, it can also affect internal organs and the eyes. There are over 1 million people under the age of 45 and 14,500 children in the UK[9] whose lives are significantly affected by their arthritis.

'All blind people want and need a guide dog.'
False . . . Guide dogs aren't always appropriate for visually impaired people and only 4,100 out of the one million registrable blind and partially sighted people have a guide dog.[10] Oh and by the way, guide dogs can't read bus numbers!

Conclusion

In the past, the myths illustrated in this article, as well as others, have been taught, and talked about, as truths. They have supported the discrimination that disabled people have experienced. These myths need to be shown for what they are, invalid. The simple fact that you have read this information will help to achieve this.

On a large scale, the myths surrounding disabled people need to be exposed within all levels of life. By working together, we can achieve this.

References
[1] The Employers Forum on Disability
[2] The Royal National Institute for Deaf People
[3] Royal National Institute for the Blind survey, 1991
[4] Mind report, 1995
[5] Joseph Rowntree Foundation, 1996
[6] Institute of Actuaries, 1993
[7] *General Household Survey: Carers in 1990*, OPCS
[8] Disability Alliance 1997
[9] Arthritis Care 1996
[10] Royal National Institute for the Blind survey, 1991

Take up thy bed and work

Harriet Harman, the Social Security Secretary, says that disabled people must not be condemned to a life of dependence on state benefits

A nation-wide debate on reforming the welfare state's help and support for people with disabilities or long-term health problems is long overdue. This Government has the opportunity and the mandate to reform the welfare state, so that it provides proper help and support in order to allow those people who can work to do so, while helping those who cannot work to live independently and with dignity.

Today's welfare state fails on both counts. Many people with disabilities are unable to work because the system neither helps nor encourages them to, and for those who cannot work – the people for whom support is most crucial – the system presents a bewildering and complex web of benefits and services.

The very complexity leaves the system open to fraud. Not only does the system not work, but it is also subject to ever-spiralling costs. It is currently costing nearly £24 billion – 25 per cent of all social security spending, up from 11 per cent in 1979.

The previous government appeared to be happy to see growing numbers of people with disabilities or health problems being written off to a life of dependence on benefits. Ministers didn't seem to care that people didn't want to be written off, or that the benefit bill was making ever-increasing demands on the public purse. For them, it was a convenient way of hiding the true scale of worklessness in Britain.

The fact is that, under the previous government, the welfare system lost touch with the real aspirations and needs of disabled people. The welfare system was still operating on a model where disability meant dependency and institutionalisation.

Disabled people did not accept that model; indeed, they had been actively challenging it for many years.

They demanded the right to be able to live independently, not in institutions. And now they want us to help them with the next step – to focus on their abilities by helping them into work.

We will not take benefits away from those who need them. But we will change the system to deliver more effective help to those for whom it's intended

---

And I agree with them. People are asking me to guarantee that there will be no changes. I'm not going to guarantee that. Indeed, I believe that change is essential. The system we have got at the moment is failing many of the people it is supposed to help. I want to reform the welfare system so that it concentrates on people's abilities, not their disabilities; extending opportunities, not trapping them on benefits – and focusing support where it is needed most.

We are determined to make sure that all government agencies (as well as local government, the NHS and voluntary organisations) work together to provide the kind of integrated support that is necessary to enable disabled people to lead the lives they want to. It's not just money that matters. Access to care and opportunities to work are also important for many disabled people in Britain today.

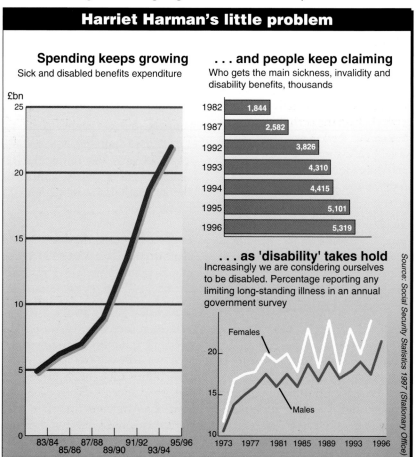

Harriet Harman's little problem

Spending keeps growing
Sick and disabled benefits expenditure

. . . and people keep claiming
Who gets the main sickness, invalidity and disability benefits, thousands

Year	Thousands
1982	1,844
1987	2,582
1992	3,826
1993	4,310
1994	4,415
1995	5,101
1996	5,319

. . . as 'disability' takes hold
Increasingly we are considering ourselves to be disabled. Percentage reporting any limiting long-standing illness in an annual government survey

Source: Social Security Statistics 1997 (Stationary Office)

We are already changing things for the better. We are committed to breaking down the barriers which prevent disabled people from playing a full role in society – by enforcing tough anti-discrimination legislation, and giving disabled people real civil rights. And we have already made £195 million available through this Government's 'New Deal' to support innovative and pioneering schemes to give disabled people new opportunities to work.

We are making these changes because we are determined to support

We are committed to breaking down the barriers which prevent disabled people from playing a full role in society

the most vulnerable and needy in society. Achieving our objectives will enable us to deliver a better welfare

state – one that does not consign people to a life on benefits at the margins of society but offers them opportunity, independence and compassion.

We will not take benefits away from those who need them. But we will change the system to deliver more effective help to those for whom it's intended. This Labour Government will reform the welfare state to work for sick and disabled people, not against them.

© *Telegraph Group Limited, London 1998*

Benefits fraud by the disabled reaches £500m

By David Fletcher, Health Correspondent

Eleven per cent of people who claim Disability Living Allowance do so fraudulently at a cost to the taxpayer of almost £500 million a year, the National Audit Office says today.

An investigation by Sir John Bourn, Comptroller and Auditor General, found most fraud was by claimants who overstated their needs or who failed to report improvements in their conditions.

Their dishonesty added up to wrongful claims costing £499 million, equivalent to 13 per cent of the total amount spent on Disability Living Allowance.

The figures, which will reinforce the Government's determination to reform benefits for disabled people, are contained in Sir John's annual examination of the Department of Social Security's accounts.

He refused fully to certify the accounts – for the ninth year running – because of the level of benefit fraud and the level of error in benefit awards, principally in Income Support and the new Jobseeker's Allowance.

Disability Living Allowance, claimed by more than 1,850,000

people at a total cost of £4,514 million, is worth up to £49.50 a week.

Independent adjudication resulted in reduction or cessation of benefit in more than half of cases where fraud was suspected, suggesting that 'borderline' fraud caused the loss of a further £70 million a year.

Sir John says: 'On the other hand, the review also estimated that there were potential underpayments of £227 million because claimants were understating their needs.'

An investigation found most fraud was by claimants who overstated their needs or who failed to report improvements in their conditions

He says the Benefits Agency is now re-examining about 450,000 people's entitlement to claim Disability Living Allowance and expects to secure savings of £67 million over two years.

An investigation by the agency's staff found that only 81 per cent of assessments for Income Support – claimed for 4.8 million people – were correct. The result of these errors by staff was that overpayments cost £337 million and underpayments amounted to £127 million.

Fraud was found in 11 per cent of a random sample of 4,350 Income Support cases examined by investigators.

Sir John says: 'Extrapolated to a national level this represents some 665,000 cases and an annual potential expenditure loss of £1.77 billion on Income Support, equivalent to around 11 per cent of expenditure.'

He recognises that the Benefits Agency is taking steps to combat fraud and improve the accuracy of payments.

'However, I continue to be concerned by the level of error in benefit awards, particularly Income Support and Jobseeker's Allowance. I share the agency's concern at the scale of benefit fraud, which presents a major challenge to the agency and the Department of Social Security.' © *Telegraph Group Limited, London 1998*

How the cuts would disable us

The government benefit review isn't just about getting disabled 'malingerers' back to work, it is a direct attack upon the right of disabled people to live independently. The world is organised to exclude disabled people from full and equal participation. The non-means-tested Disability Living Allowance (DLA) is provided to meet the additional costs of disability resulting from these forms of social exclusion.

I am registered blind and receive the low rate mobility and medium rate care components of DLA. I am in full-time work but (despite my relatively high wage) find it difficult to meet my additional daily living and mobility costs without help.

DLA helps me pay for someone to do my washing, cleaning, shopping and home administration, assists me to contribute towards the welfare of others through voluntary social work and for social contact with my friends and family. I spend £340 per month on the additional costs of disability, approximately £180 of which is covered by DLA.

Because I am blind, I am not eligible for community care services. Budget constraints force the council to prioritise disabled people it perceives to be in greater need. Were the DLA to be subject to means testing, I would most certainly lose all entitlement to it.

Kirsten Hearn.
London N4.

The Social Security Bill currently going through Parliament implements major cuts in benefit rights for people with disabilities. In particular:

- The bill abolishes disability appeal tribunals. These were established in 1992 to hear appeals against decisions relating to disability benefits. One of their major strengths is that they have to include a member who has knowledge or experience of disability;

- The bill restricts back-dated entitlement of disability and other benefits to one month. This will particularly hit disabled people because they are least likely to have access to information and advice about their entitlements.

Unfortunately, when the bill went before the House of Commons, the only clause to receive any attention was that relating to lone parents.

David Simmons.
118A Edward Road,
London E17 6NX.

I am a disabled person whose benefits are currently under review in the Benefits Integrity project (through which you receive a 33-page questionnaire or a visit from an official to see if you are still eligible for your benefits). I will be uneasy, to say the least, over the festive period.

To get my DLA in the first place, I went to appeal stage, which was the most humiliating experience of my life. I was cross-examined like a criminal. However, I was awarded the middle rate care and higher rate mobility component of the DLA for life. The questionnaire I have now received belies this – as it is essentially a new claim form.

My DLA enabled me to make huge differences in my life. I learned to drive an adapted vehicle, became mobile, and use the care allowance to pay people to help in my home. This means I can use what limited energy I have on full-time work. I have moved away from dependency on family and friends and taken up a job in a different part of the country. I am paying in to my pension scheme.

Does the fact that I currently work mean that I should automatically be herded into the not in 'genuine need' category Tony Blair speaks of for disability benefits?

Jenny Mitchell.
15 Chapman Avenue,
Derby DE24 0GN.

As a practising solicitor, chairman of the disability charity, John Grooms, and a wheelchair user, I am increasingly worried about the

BENEFIT REVIEW

'behind closed doors' approach of welfare reform for people with disabilities, from a government led by a party which prides itself on the importance of democracy.

It seems as if we are returning to those dark Dickensian days where people are valued solely in terms of their ability to work, rather than looking forward to an era where disabled people are valued as people first.

David Thompson.
50 Scrutton Street,
London EC2A 4PH.

There is nothing like a big dose of pious hypocrisy to round off Christmas. The Prime Minister thinks it appalling that social security spending is bigger than the health, education and policing budget combined. He might consider, whilst he genuflects before the Prince of Peace this Christmas, that the budget for the Trident missile programme is bigger than all of them combined.

John Medhurst.
126 Montgomery Street,
Hove, Sussex.

David Brindle is indeed to be congratulated on being named 'Journalist of the Year' for revealing the Tories' secret cuts in war pensions. A much greater accolade awaits him were he to be able to reveal what hard choices our Dear Leader has in mind for them.

Brian M Leahy.
7 Stocks Lane, Abingdon,
Oxon OX13 6SG.

A Private Member's bill to re-assert a fundamental right for disabled people, has just passed from the Lords to the Commons. The bill, sponsored by Lord Ashley of Stoke, seeks to ensure that disabled people's services are determined by their assessed needs.

Earlier this year the Law Lords ruled, in a case brought by Gloucester County Council, that the local authority could take its own ability to pay into consideration when establishing levels of service. Lord Ashley's bill seeks to amend the 1970 Chronically Sick and Disabled Persons Act to re-establish disabled people's needs as the first priority. It is important that it receives the support of MPs.

Bob Benson.
Director, Disability Scotland,
Princes House,
Edinburgh EH2 4RG.
© The Guardian
December, 1997

Totting up bill for illness and disability

How many people get it?
4.3 million get the general sickness and disability benefits. Some people can claim disability premium on top of income support.

How much does it cost?
The disability bill has trebled since the early 1980s from £4.1bn (£7bn in today's prices) to £23.5bn. It is now one-quarter of the social security budget.

What types of benefit are there?
The main benefits are Incapacity benefits (a means-tested benefit for people who are unable to work short- or long-term), Disability Living Allowance, Attendance Allowance, Severe Disablement Allowance, Invalid Care Allowance, Industrial Injuries Allowance, war pensions.

Who gets what?
1.9 million get Disability Living Allowance, which is split into two components: mobility (£13.50-£34.60 per week) and care (£13.50-£49.50).

How about paying for care?
Attendance Allowance is a tax-free benefit for help with care ranging from £32.40 to £48.50.

What if I'm disabled through work?
You are eligible for Industrial Injuries Benefit, claimed by a quarter of a million people.

Who pays?
The Government, if there is no blame attached to the company for your disablement.

What if I haven't paid enough National Insurance to qualify for incapacity benefit?
You get Severe Disablement Allowance, which is tax free. Again you have to take the All Work Test.

What if I can't work?
You may be eligible for Incapacity Benefit – 2.4 million get it. Short-term is £47.10 a week, long-term £55.70. To get this benefit people have to take the All Work Test – which involves a doctor assessing your ability to work, sit, lift and stand in addition to any injuries or ailments you may have. The scoring system means anyone with 15 points or more on a 0-30 scale remains in benefit.

What if I am working?
12,500 get Disability Working Allowance – those working for low wages or short hours get £49.55 single £77.55 for a couple.

Why has the bill gone up so much?
A combination of factors:
1. A push in the early 1990s to alert people that they could claim such benefits.
2. An ageing population needs more care.
3. There were suggestions that some people may have been shunted on to incapacity benefit rather than stay on the unemployment count, and that some GPs were sympathetic to putting people on benefit. Incapacity Benefit, with its All Work Test, was introduced in April 1995 to try to stop this.

© The Independent
December, 1997

£10bn disabled benefit 'goes to the better-off'

By David Hughes, Political Editor

As protests by disabled campaigners reached the gates of Downing Street yesterday, the Government claimed that £10 billion a year in disability benefits is paid to better-off households.

The immense figure will strengthen Tony Blair's hand as he confronts cabinet critics of his welfare reforms.

And yesterday Chancellor Gordon Brown threw down the gauntlet to the Labour rebels, declaring: 'The true defenders of the welfare state are those who are prepared to reform it.'

Mr Blair's warning that multiplying numbers of claimants mean 'no one with an ounce of sense could look at those facts and not think that we need to change' expresses what a number of senior politicians have believed for some time – that far too many people are exploiting the disability benefit system as the richest milk cow in the welfare state.

According to official Department of Social Security statistics, 40 per cent of the £24 billion paid out each year in disability and incapacity benefits goes to households with above average incomes.

And about £3.5billion of that is paid to the 25 per cent of families rated as having the highest incomes in Britain. That covers single adults earning more than £20,000 a year or two-parent families with an income of more than £27,000 a year.

The reason is that most disability benefits are not means tested. They are paid out to anyone who meets the disability tests on the long-standing grounds that the welfare state should treat everyone the same. Even mobile phones can be arranged for those who qualify for the right state-aided disability packages.

The figures were leaked yesterday to head off the political backlash triggered by Government plans to curb the soaring cost of disability benefits.

The Prime Minister, in his Durham constituency of Sedgefield, said it was 'nonsense' to suggest the benefits review clashed with his Christian beliefs.

> ***Spending on sickness and disability benefits has grown from £4.1 billion in 1982 to £23.5 billion this year – a quarter of all welfare spending***

'What we have to do is make sure those who are genuinely in need get the help they want because the system at the moment is failing them. We have poverty increasing as the bills are rising.' He insisted that at the same time as helping those genuinely in need, the Government had to reform the system 'so that we don't carry on spending more and more money and getting less and less for it because our schools, hospitals

and transport system also require spending'.

The figures, officially published next month, break down spending on sickness and disability benefits which has grown from £4.1billion in 1982 to £23.5billion this year – a quarter of all welfare spending. At least 4.3 million people receive some such benefit.

The two most expensive – the Disability Living Allowance, which costs the taxpayer £4.4billion, and the Incapacity Benefit, costing £7.8billion – have been highlighted by those campaigning against cuts as particularly vulnerable to the Blair reforms.

Shadow Chancellor Peter Lilley accused the Government of simply trying to make cuts, rather than weed out those who should not be claiming. 'We believe you should not cut the amount going to individual disabled people, but try to stop it going to people who are not genuinely disabled or could be helped back into work.'

Gordon Brown joined the fray with an interview for today's *Times*.

He insisted: 'The welfare state is failing millions of people who depend upon it and at the same time millions who contribute towards it. The war on poverty, which is what we are fighting, was never won by the old methods.'

The Chancellor insisted that the wide-ranging review of welfare, which ministers believe could last for a decade, was not 'cuts driven'.

'To say that it is an indiscriminate slash-and-burn exercise is completely wrong. This is inspired by the need to restore the welfare state to its original purpose of opportunity and security for all. The war on poverty can only be won by the modernisers.'

Are you disabled?

A guide to benefits if you are disabled. Information from the Department of Social Security

The benefit enquiry line

A confidential telephone service is available for people with disabilities and their carers. Ring the Benefit Enquiry Line (BEL) 0800 88 22 00. People with speech or hearing problems using a textphone can dial 0800 24 33 55.

The person taking your call will not have your personal papers but will be able to give you general advice. This advice must not be taken as a decision on any matter about which you are making an enquiry.

Disability Living Allowance (DLA)

This is a tax-free benefit for people who need help with personal care, with getting around or both. It is:

- not dependent on National Insurance contributions
- not affected by any savings or (usually) by any income you and your partner may have
- usually ignored as income for Income Support or Jobseeker's Allowance claims
- for people who start to need help when they are under 65.

For people who become disabled on or after age 65, Attendance Allowance is available for those needing care.

There are two components to DLA:

The **care component**, if you need help with personal care because you are ill or disabled.

- For example for things like washing, dressing, using the toilet. If you are 16 or over this can include preparing a cooked main meal. You can get DLA even if no one is actually giving you the care you need.

The **mobility component**, if you need help with getting around.

- If you are 5 or over and can't walk at all or have difficulty in walking because you are ill or disabled. And you can get it if you can

walk but need someone with you to make sure you are safe or to help you find your way around most of the time.

To get DLA you must normally have needed help for at least three months and be likely to need it for at least a further six months. Some people suffer from a terminal illness. There are special rules for them so that they can get benefit quickly and easily.

Getting paid under the special rules means:

- getting £49.50 each week for help with personal care, whether or not you need any help
- getting paid straight away. There is no need to wait until you have needed help for three months
- claims are dealt with more quickly.

But you can only get money for help with getting around if you have difficulties with getting around.

- The special rules apply to people who may not live longer than six months because of an illness. But it is, of course, impossible to say exactly how long a person will live.

How to claim DLA

You can get a claim pack by filling in and sending off the tear-off slip from leaflet DS704 *Disability Living Allowance*, which you can get from a social security office.

More information

See leaflets DS704 *Disability Living Allowance* and HB6 *A practical guide for disabled people*. DS704 is also available in Bengali, Chinese, Greek, Gujarati, Hindi, Punjabi, Turkish, Urdu, Vietnamese and Welsh.

Other help

If you are 16 or over and working at least 16 hours a week you may be

Estimates of the prevalence of disability

The overall prevalence rate is 197 per thousand in 1996/97, compared with the 1985 survey estimate of 135 per thousand

Age group	1985	1996/97
	(rate per thousand)	
16-19	21	53
20-24	27	53
25-29	31	54
30-34	40	79
35-39	44	93
40-44	59	113
45-49	79	139
50-54	106	193
55-59	155	295
60-64	205	268
65-69	275	296
70-74	342	334
75-79	466	645
80-84	616	708
85+	779	831
All 16 and over	135	197

Source: Martin and others (1998) for 1985; FRS Follw-Up Survey of Disability for 1996/97

able to get Disability Working Allowance. You can get claim pack DWA1 from your social security office.

If you get DLA you may also get Christmas Bonus.

You can't get DLA if your need for help with personal care started on or after your 65th birthday. You may be able to get Attendance Allowance instead.

Attendance Allowance

This is a tax-free weekly cash benefit for people aged 65 or over who need help with personal care because of an illness or disability. It is:
- not dependent on National Insurance contributions
- not affected by any savings or (usually) by any income you and your partner may have
- usually ignored as income for Income Support or Jobseeker's Allowance claims.

To get Attendance Allowance (AA) you must normally have needed help with personal care for six months. You can get AA even if no one is actually giving you the care you need. Some people suffer from a terminal illness. There are special rules for them so that they can get benefit quickly and easily.

Getting paid under the special rules means:
- getting £49.50 each week for help with personal care, whether or not you need help
- getting paid straight away. There is no need to wait until you have needed help for six months
- claims are dealt with more quickly.

People who:
are under age 65 *and* need help with personal care, or help with getting around, or both, should claim Disability Living Allowance (DLA).

How to claim Attendance Allowance
Use the form in leaflet DS702 *Attendance Allowance*, which you can get from social security offices.

More information
See leaflet DS702 *Attendance Allowance*. It is also available in Bengali, Chinese, Greek, Gujarati, Hindi, Punjabi, Turkish, Urdu, Vietnamese and Welsh.

Other help
If you get Attendance Allowance you may also get Christmas Bonus.
- The special rules apply to people who may not live longer than six months because of an illness. But it is, of course, impossible to say exactly how long a person will live.

Disability Working Allowance (DWA)

This is a tax-free, income-related benefit for people aged 16 or over who are working 16 hours a week or more on average and have an illness or disability that limits their earning capacity.

Your right to DWA does not depend on National Insurance contributions.

Who can get DWA?
To get DWA you must be 16 or over **and** be working for 16 hours a week or more on average and have an illness or disability that puts you at a disadvantage in getting a job **and** you must also either be getting:
Disability Living Allowance
or Attendance Allowance
or War Disablement Pension with War Pensioner's Constant Attendance Allowance or mobility supplement
or Industrial Injuries Disablement Benefit with Constant Attendance Allowance
or have an invalid three-wheeler supplied from the DSS
or for at least one of the 56 days before you claim you must have been getting short-term Incapacity Benefit paid at the higher rate, long-term Incapacity Benefit, Severe Disablement Allowance, or a disability premium or a higher pensioner premium with either Income Support, income-based Jobseeker's Allowance, Housing Benefit, or Council Tax Benefit.

You can get DWA if you are employed or self-employed, but you will not get it if you are on a training scheme getting a training allowance.

You can't get DWA if you, or you and your partner together, have savings of more than £16,000. Any savings you have between £3,000 and £16,000 will affect the amount of DWA you can get.

If you were getting short-term Incapacity Benefit paid at the higher rate, long-term Incapacity Benefit, or Severe Disablement Allowance before you started work and began getting DWA, you may go back to your old benefit if, within two years, you are still getting DWA but have to give up your job and are incapable of work.

The disability test
For a first claim you will be asked to read the leaflet in the DWA claim pack, which lists the circumstances that enable you to pass the disability test. If you then decide that you could pass the test, you need only sign a simple declaration that your illness or disability puts you at a disadvantage in getting a job.

For renewal claims, a further declaration will be needed, and you may also have to fill in a self-assessment form which lists some illnesses and disabilities that could put you at a disadvantage in getting a job. We will ask for confirmation of your assessment from a professional involved in your care. Only rarely will a medical examination be necessary.

How much you get
The amount of money depends on whether you have a partner, how many children you have living with you and their ages, and how much money you, or you and your partner together, have coming in each week. DWA is paid at the same rate for 26 weeks. The amount will normally stay the same even if your income or other circumstances change during that period.

You may also be able to get some of the cost of your childcare charges taken into account when your benefit is calculated.

You may also get more DWA if you are working 30 hours or more a week.

How to claim DWA
Contact your social security office for a claim form. Do not delay in making your claim or you may lose benefit.

More information
See leaflet DS703 *Disability Working*

Allowance – the cash benefit for disabled people in work, available from your social security office or Jobcentre. This leaflet is also available in Bengali, Chinese, Greek, Gujarati, Hindi, Punjabi, Turkish, Urdu, Vietnamese and Welsh. Ask for DS703 in the language you want. There are audio cassettes in these and other languages.

See also leaflet HB4 *A guide to Disability Working Allowance* for details of other qualifying conditions, or ask at your social security office.

Other help

If you get DWA you may also be able to get:

- help with your rent
- help with your council tax
- help with health costs
- a Social Fund Maternity Payment
- help with the cost of prison visits – ask at your social security office.

Income Support or Jobseeker's Allowance may be available for people who:

– are working 16 hours a week or more **and** have a mental or physical disability

– if because of that disability they are able to earn only 75 per cent or less of what a person without that disability would be expected to earn.

Child support maintenance

The Child Support Agency (CSA) is responsible for child support maintenance.

If you are living with and caring for a child and one, or both, of the child's parents are living elsewhere in the UK you may apply to have child support maintenance assessed and collected by the CSA. If you or your present partner claim Income Support, income-based Jobseeker's Allowance, Family Credit or Disability Working Allowance, you may be required to apply for child support maintenance if asked to do so by the CSA.

More information

Get leaflet CSA2001 *For parents who live apart* from a social security office, or phone the Child Support Agency National Enquiry Line on 0345 133 133 (lines are open 9am – 5pm Monday to Friday).

Child Maintenance Bonus

If you get child support maintenance and leave Income Support or income-based Jobseeker's Allowance because you or your partner start work, increase hours, or increase earnings, you could qualify for a Child Maintenance Bonus. For more information contact your social security office.

Free milk for disabled children

If you have a child aged between 5 and 16 who is so disabled, either mentally or physically, that he or she cannot attend any school, you can get tokens to exchange for seven pints (or eight half-litres) of liquid milk each week for him or her. You do not have to be in receipt of any social security benefits. You will need to fill in form FW20. For a copy of this form write to:

Family Credit Helpline
Room A106D
Government Buildings
Cop Lane
Penwortham
Preston PR1 0SA

Injured by crime

If you are injured as a result of a crime of violence you can claim criminal injuries compensation.

For your application to be considered, you must have been physically and/or mentally injured as a result of a crime of violence and injured seriously enough to qualify

for at least a minimum award of £1,000. You may also qualify if you are a dependant or relative of a victim of a crime of violence who has since died.

The amount of award depends on the severity of the injuries sustained.

More information

For more information contact the: Criminal Injuries Compensation Authority
Tay House
300 Bath Street
Glasgow G2 4JR
Tel: 0141 331 2726.

Vaccine damage

If you have been severely disabled as a result of vaccination you may be able to get a one-off, tax-free payment, currently £30,000.

The scheme covers vaccination against diphtheria, tetanus, whooping cough, tuberculosis, poliomyelitis, measles, rubella (German measles), mumps, and Haemophilus influenzae type b (Hib).

More information

See leaflet HB3 *Payment for people severely disabled by a vaccine* or write to:
Vaccine Damage Payments Unit
Palatine House
Lancaster Road
Preston PR1 1HB.

© *Department of Social Security*
June, 1998

Disabled demand end to 'apartheid'

By Glenda Cooper, Social Affairs Correspondent

The Prime Minister was yesterday urged to help more children with learning disabilities integrate into mainstream schools, as campaigners called for an end to 'apartheid' against disabled people.

Young people presented a letter to Tony Blair at Downing Street yesterday asking him to support a change in the law stopping local education authorities forcing disabled children into special schools.

Among the group were disabled youngsters fighting legislation to join friends and siblings in ordinary schools.

While the law says society should not discriminate, Rights Now, the group which campaigns for civil rights for disabled people, says it does not always work in practice. Rachel Hurst, chairman of the group, says: 'It's a kind of apartheid – we've been saying that for years. All the other things we have to put up with, being spat on, patronised and ignored are just the icing on the gingerbread.'

A survey by Britain's leading disability care charity, the Leonard Cheshire, recently revealed that almost a third of the public believe those in wheelchairs are 'less intelligent'. More than half said they have no contact with the disabled although one in ten people have a disability. Last week the Royal National Institute for the Blind revealed that among older blind or partially sighted people, nine out of ten have an income less than half of the national average and half were living on a weekly household income of less than £150.

'Imagine having to cope on an income well below the poverty line. Imagine being unable to get out and visit friends and family, go to the pub or even to the local shop,' said Ian Bruce, RNIB's director general. 'That is the harsh reality for hundreds of thousands of older people in the UK – because they have a sight problem. It is quite simply a national scandal.' At present the main legislation is the two-year-old Disability Discrimination Act. 'It is the only protection we have, but it has no enforcement mechanism,' said Ms Hurst. 'And we can't afford to go to court. The act doesn't cover some of the most important areas such as transport, housing and education.'

'People who are disabled face discrimination in all areas of their lives, whether it's finding a job, using the health service or going on holiday'

A ministerial task-force recommended in December that a commission be set up. This has been accepted by the Government and must be implemented by the year 2000.

'I'm not sure whether it is the discrimination so much as the thoughtlessness and lack of vision,' said Jess Clare, manager of specialist services for Jewish Care. 'But when it comes to employment there are lots of extremely intelligent people with university degrees who can't get jobs.'

A spokesman for Mencap said that people with learning disabilities face similar prejudice. 'People who are disabled face discrimination in all areas of their lives, whether it's finding a job, using the health service or going on holiday. There is a lack of understanding about what they can achieve. People can live independently with the right support.

'There is still much to be done.

SORRY, WE'RE LOOKING FOR SOMEONE TALLER

UK PLC APPOINTMENTS BOARD

KenPyne

Last year a Mencap group going to the Costa del Sol was not allowed to board a plane because the pilot said it wasn't safe.'

'The Government has given a manifesto to provide "dignity and security in retirement", said Barbara Scott, manager of a residential RNIB home in Somerset. 'However for older blind and partially sighted people, dignity and security are luxuries enjoyed by the small minority. Additional resources are needed on a major scale to tackle what is undoubtedly a national scandal.

'Long-term reform to pensions and the funding of social care will not meet the challenge which is immediate, urgent and real.'

Ronald Taylor

Having an obvious physical disability makes you an easy target for the prejudiced. But having a less obvious one, or a mental disability, can leave you just as open to discrimination.

Ronald Taylor suffers from hearing impairment and learning disabilities. He used to work in a leather factory making handbags and shoes. When the firm closed he found it impossible to get another job.

Not that he'd been treated that well when he was employed. Despite his ability to carry out skilled work, he was made to do the menial tasks: 'I was always the one who was made to run up and down everywhere, get everyone's breakfast, it was always my turn to make the tea. It hurt to be talked to as if I was a little kid, as if these were the jobs that I should do,' he says.

Apart from people taking advantage of his learning disabilities, Ronald encountered lack of sympathy because of his hearing problems: 'A lot of people don't understand when you're hard of hearing, that it's not that you're stupid, you just haven't heard what they said. They'll get in a temper with you and start to shout at you and it's not your fault. Say if I'm on the telephone and I have to ask someone to speak up they get really annoyed.'

He has felt lonely and isolated, although he tries to maintain a cheerful outlook. 'Since my mother died no one in the family has had anything to do with me. They don't

want to see me or speak to me in case I'm asking for something. They assume I want money. All I want is a bit of understanding.'

Coral McKenzie

Coral McKenzie is thinking of giving up trying to get a job, after a string of job interviews in which people saw her disability first and her abilities second.

'People look at you with their mouths open and the first thing that pops into their mind is the mobility problem. They think "you're no good because you're not mobile",' she says.

Coral, 32, from East London, had a stroke at the age of 21. 'I just cried and cried. It was months of crying and I realised it was turning into years of crying. I began to think I was going mad.'

Before the stroke she had worked in the Post Office. She has taken a number of computer courses. Her attempts to use these skills in the workplace to help herself and others have met with failure.

'Just because you're not as mobile [as others] they don't care if you can do something as well as, if not better than, someone else,' she says. 'The last interview I went to, the man turned round to me and said: "We would have given it to you it's just that we need someone who is mobile for the job."

'This was a desk-bound job with computer. There was no moving around needed. I'd rather that he had just been honest and said: "I can't cope with you being disabled."'

She now begins to think that she will not be trying again, 'You get so many knock backs, you think can I be bothered? How many more times can I take this?'

She feels the disabled are treated as second-class citizens, even by those who are meant to help them: 'Housing is hell. I waited two years to have a shower installed that I could use. I rang up the council and they said they'd closed my file. I said: "Hello, I'm not dead. I'm still alive."'

For tranport she has to rely on taxis. 'I've attempted public transport but it's dreadful,' she said. 'Trains are usually better as there's at least someone to help you on and off.'

Christine Dance

Christine Dance suffers from arthritis and for the last six years has been forced to use a wheelchair. As soon as she stopped being able to walk she noticed a change in the way people treated her.

'They suddenly started to talk down to me,' she says. 'They look right through you and address the next person in the queue.'

If she tries to make her presence felt the reaction is as hurtful: 'They look at you as if you were from another planet. I want to say "Do you think I've got two heads or something?"'

Since her illness things she used to take for granted have become impossible. 'Public transport has been so hard. It's not really possible to use public transport if you're disabled.'

Her home had to be modified: 'I had to wait for about a year and a half before my home was done. I think I was lucky I only had to wait that long, as the housing trust is pretty good.'

'What I miss is things like not being able to go to the pictures because so many cinemas have stairs.'

She now works as a receptionist at a Leonard Cheshire day centre in east London. 'I was a housewife before I became disabled but trying to get into the workplace if you are disabled is dreadful,' she said. 'It's like a vicious circle – you don't see any disabled people [in a firm] so none can get in.'

She says the most difficult thing has been the reaction of family and friends: 'My next door neighbour accused me of faking once. I was so shocked. And as for my family I don't hear from them.'

© *The Independent*
May, 1998

If you think disabled people get a raw deal

You're not alone

It's hard enough being disabled. But the lives of severely disabled men, women and children in the United Kingdom are made even more difficult by extreme financial hardship.

If you are disabled, you'll already know all about the problems, But what if you are fit and healthy?

Can you begin to imagine what would become of you and your family if you had a serious accident or illness, resulting in disability?

Contrary to popular belief, state benefits hardly come close to providing a reasonable standard of living. Let alone a few luxuries.

And the rest of your family? They'd have to suffer the effects of your disability as well. At the very least their quality of life would be much diminished. Almost certainly, you'd find bills for the essentials of life piling up far quicker than you could ever hope to pay them

And then what . . . Join DIG, join the campaign for a disability income.

What is DIG?

The Disablement Income Group. We were founded in 1965 by two disabled women. Their aim was to create an organisation capable of influencing government policy towards disabled people.

In 1972 DIG reached the conclusion that all severely disabled people should receive a disability income which would enable families to stay together and be free from the threat of poverty.

Has DIG been successful?

Up to a point. We were instrumental in securing the introduction of several important benefits:

- Attendance allowance – for people needing a lot of looking after. For people aged 65 and

under, this allowance is now known as Disability Living Allowance.
- Invalidity pensions – for people who had worked but were no longer able to do so due to long-term disability. This was replaced by incapacity benefit in 1995.
- A non-contributory invalidity pension (NCIP) – for people too ill or disabled to work, who had paid enough National Insurance contributions. This is now known as severe disablement allowance.

And we won recognition of the importance for severely disabled people of being able to live independently in the community when in 1988 we were asked by the government to establish the Independent Living Fund in co-operation with the Department of Social Security. The Fund had a fixed tern of five years and has now closed. But during its lifetime it helped thousands of severely disabled people employ their own carers in their own

homes. A successor fund continues making payments to all beneficiaries of the old Fund.

Good news, bad news

Despite all these improvements, the vast majority of severely disabled people continue to lead a hand-to-mouth existence.

Financial assistance from the state still falls far below needs. In fact, there is ample evidence suggesting that the government is only just beginning to understand what those needs are, let alone the costs involved.

Tinkering with the social security system is not the answer.

Achieving our goal

Our research indicates that the cost of disability can account for 47% of a severely disabled person's household budget.

This 'disability tax' means there is less cash for ordinary everyday expenses. As a result, it is not uncommon for disabled people to have to choose between adequate heating and eating.

Disabled people need regular cash payments that will help to meet their extra costs.

They also need to replace the earnings most of them lose because of their disabilities.

In short, a national disability income. But will we ever win the right to a national disability income?

Can we see an end to the humiliation suffered by disabled people because they do not have enough money to live on?

We believe that the voice of disabled people is still not being heard. Even though there are at least five million disabled people in this country, most politicians of all persuasions feel they can safely ignore us.

We are not a vote-catching issue. At least, not yet. We know that five million people acting together can make a lot of noise.

Such a group would be far too large, far too vociferous, far too active, to be ignored.

Take action now
Join DIG

Join DIG if you are disabled. Join DIG if you are not disabled and want to add your voice and add weight to our campaign. Of course, we need cash to fund our work. But that's not why we are asking you to join. We want to know who you are, what your needs are. That way, we are armed with factual, statistical, irrefutable evidence to move the government of the day.

But what can DIG do?
We are experienced campaigners. We have well-known and active supporters in and out of Parliament. We have regular contact with policy makers. We understand how policy is made, and how it can be influenced. By having more members, we can exert more pressure. The needs of disabled people have sympathy right across the political spectrum.

It's our task to convert that often stated sympathy into long overdue, meaningful action.

What else does DIG do?
We provide an advisory service for disabled people and their families. We offer practical guidance and assistance – especially in explaining what benefits can be claimed, by whom, and how much.

There are thousands of disabled people whom we have helped to obtain increases in benefits – simply by knowing how to go about claiming, what to claim for, and how to appeal against an initial refusal.

We offer an information service, keeping subscribers up to date with the latest news and developments. We also publish a journal that keeps members informed about our campaigns and activities.

So help us to help you. Join DIG today.

© The Disablement Income Group (DIG)
June, 1998

Should disability benefit be cut?

For
Tony Blair is right in looking at ways to reduce welfare payouts. There are too many so-called disabled collecting considerable amounts when they are able to work. I know two scroungers living the life of Riley in Spain, playing golf every day, all on disability payouts from the UK. Both are able to work – they can do everything else, walk, drive, lift, gardening etc.

Now they discover they can claim even more by citing their wives as carers – collecting allowances on this pretext and even claiming as much as £6,000 in back allowances. These men are still only in their early 50s.

They manage to hoodwink some Spanish doctor into signing the necessary documents and hey-presto, the British taxpayer is conned again. Genuine cases of disability should be helped, but too many scroungers are milking the system.

More strength to Mr Blair's elbow – it's time something was done about this.

Mrs J. K. Saunders, Orpington, Kent.

Against
My pet fly was resting on a wall in 10 Downing Street recently when it overheard this conversation between the Prime Minister and Social Security Secretary.

Blair: How is our project progressing?

Harman: Very well, Tony. I predict that in 12 months the Disability Living Allowance and ancillary benefits will be terminated.

Blair: Well done – but what about all those old people who are genuinely disabled?

Harman: Don't worry, Tony. The shock of being told their benefits are being stopped will kill them off. If any commit suicide we stand to make two gains; no more disability allowances and fewer pensions.

Blair: Clever girl, Harriet. In any case, I shall be introducing a Bill soon to recommend putting down anyone over 75 (except politicians and judges, of course). We're Young England now.

At this point, my fly flew off, and I heard him buzz: 'Lords what fools these voters be.'

G. Caborn, Swansea.
© The Daily Mail
December, 1997

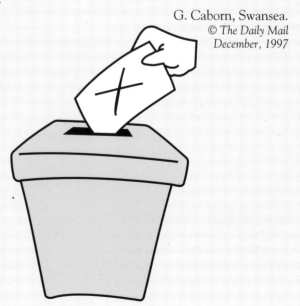

Cash-in-hand scheme set to stall in the blocks

David Brindle on the patchy preparation for direct payments to the disabled.

Next week sees the culmination of a 30-year campaign by disabled people to take control of their personal care arrangements.

But the event looks like being marked by more of a whimper than a bang.

From next Tuesday, local authorities will be able to give disabled people the cash to buy their own care instead of providing them with direct services. The aim is to improve people's choice and control, while cutting costs and bureaucracy: according to one study, savings could be up to 40 per cent.

If the scheme works well, it may be extended to elderly care. In this month's social services white paper, the Conservatives said they would review progress after a year and extend it to 'other categories of service user'. Labour is also keen on the idea in principle.

However, it is doubtful there will be much to review after 12 months. Preparations for direct payments can at best be termed patchy, with no more than half of all authorities making plans, and the Department of Health's own guidelines for the scheme have yet to appear.

Jane Campbell, co-director of the National Centre for Independent Living, set up to advise and assist on direct payments, says: 'The ignorance among the authorities about what to do, and how to do it, is absolutely outstanding. Some of the calls coming in are hilarious.'

Except in Scotland, it has until now been unlawful for authorities to give people money to buy services. Under the Community Care (Direct Payments) Act 1996, adults under 65 with a physical or learning disability will be the first to be eligible for such awards – though the local authority will decide whether they

get them. People who start receiving payments before age 65 will be able to carry on after.

About 2,000 people, mainly physically disabled, have been getting money indirectly from authorities under some 60 third-party schemes designed to get round the prohibition on direct payments. Thousands of disabled people have also gained experience of making their own care arrangements with grants from the Independent Living Fund (ILF).

Industrial injury

Expenditure on Industrial Injuries Disablement Benefit Total expenditure, £m

Year	£m
82/83	343
87/88	453
92/93	601
93/94	616
94/95	645
95/96	670
96/97	661

If you contract a disease or become disabled because of an accident at work, you can claim Industrial Injuries Disablement Benefit

- You must be at least '14% disabled': total loss of sight, hearing or hands counts as 100%, loss of an index finger as 14% (some assessments can be added together).

- Payments vary from £12.38 (20% disabled) to £101.10 (100%) per week

Source: Social Security Statistics 1997

An analysis by the Policy Studies Institute found that 9 in 10 local authorities would make direct payments, if allowed, and that disabled people making their own care arrangements reported greater satisfaction with results. Self-arranged services were also markedly cheaper – an average £5.18 an hour compared with £8.52 for others – although the PSI warned that the terms of carers employed by disabled people could be 'less than ideal'.

Pauline Thompson, director of the Disablement Income Group, says the prospects for direct payments are exciting and should not be clouded by the likely slow start.

She thinks it inevitable that some authorities will be concerned about the impact on their staff, that some will see the scheme as a form of privatisation and that the new English unitary social services departments – 13 of which start next week – will view it as a low priority. 'They will be wondering if they have enough money to deliver what they are supposed to be delivering, never mind direct payments,' says Thompson, pointing out that authorities have received no funding for implementing the scheme.

Campbell, whose centre is getting three years' health department backing of £80,000 a year, says the key to the scheme's success will be the involvement of local enabling groups, working with authorities and advising individuals on how to be model employers of care workers.

Harking back to what happened in early days of the ILF, Campbell says: 'What I don't want is people ending up in court because they haven't paid tax or national insurance. That's the danger.'

© *The Guardian*
March, 1997

Blighted lives

Frances Rickford on research that shows too much focus on parents' needs can be harmful

Years after the closure of the long-stay mental handicap hospitals, there are still thousands of disabled children living in institutions, many of them leading bleak and isolated lives. New research by Dr Jenny Morris for the Joseph Rowntree Foundation has found that social services for children with disabilities remain focused on their parents' need for respite, rather than on the needs and wishes of the children themselves.

Because of changes in attitudes, and the development of better community-based care services, most children and young people in institutions are now those with quite severe learning disabilities or multiple impairments. The majority live in special boarding schools, sometimes for 52 weeks a year, and many of those who do go home for the holidays spend large parts of them in other respite care facilities.

Morris and her colleagues talked to 32 disabled children and young people living away from home. They also undertook a detailed study of the way the Children Act is being implemented in respect of disabled children in three local authorities.

The study found that most children in residential placements had gone to live there before they reached the age of 10, and in one establishment run by a voluntary sector organisation more than a third of the children were under seven when their placement began. Some described their sadness and confusion at being sent away from their families at a very young age.

For example, Monica was sent to a residential school for the deaf at the age of five when she hadn't yet learned sign language. 'I was saying, "No, I want to stay home." My mum said, "No, you stay here and do your work, I'm going home," and said goodbye.'

Lenny was sent to a children's home at the age of eight. After a couple of years he returned to his family, but would go back to the children's home regularly to give his mother a break.

Lenny didn't understand why he had to go when his younger brother and sister were allowed to stay at home. He told the researcher: 'I was only eight and she couldn't control me. I mean, I am a bit of a bad lad but compared to others, what was I? I'm resentful towards my Mum because I was in a wheelchair and I was the one that had to come here.'

Some of the young people enjoyed life at their schools and residential homes, and seemed to have good relationships with their care workers. Like all children, friendship was especially important to them. Monica was taught to sign by other children at her school, and said her 'good friends' were the best thing about being there.

Others were less happy – bullied by other children or ignored by the staff. Jackie, who has very little contact with her own family and cannot speak, indicated that the worst thing about her residential home was that the staff didn't talk to her. As the residents were all dependent on the staff to help them communicate with each other, Jackie seemed to be completely isolated.

Parents were often deeply torn about allowing their children to live away from home, but found if they needed help there was little alternative. Services for disabled children are still largely 'service led' rather than 'needs led' and were not geared primarily to meeting the needs of the child but instead to helping parents cope.

Information about disabled children living away from home was haphazard and many had no allocated social worker. Social workers were confused about their responsibilities under the Children Act, and often assumed that because of a child's communication problems there would be no point in trying to ascertain their wishes, as the act requires.

Many disabled children placed in residential institutions for short or long periods clearly have very difficult and challenging care needs, including violent behaviour, hyperactivity and sleeping problems. But as Morris reports: 'Again and again this research project came across situations where the solution to difficult family circumstances was seen to be to remove the disabled child from the home.'

© *The Guardian*
April, 1998

Hello, sister! Hello, brother!

Living with a brother or a sister with disabilities

In Britain, most children with disabilities live at home with their own families. These children – an estimated 355,000 – bring a great deal to their families and are loved and valued. However, some children with special needs do require a great deal of attention and care and this can impact on the whole family – especially other brothers and sisters.

There are no easy solutions to this, and all families are different, but we hope this information will help encourage the parents, brothers and sisters of children with disabilities to talk about their needs and feelings.

Tips for children

Having a brother or sister with a disability can be wonderful. But it can also be difficult. These brothers or sisters can take up a lot of your parents' time, and you might feel left out or angry when you're not getting much attention.

I wish I had more time alone with Mum or Dad

If you feel you aren't getting enough time with your Mum or Dad, ask if some time can be set aside each day for you, perhaps after your brother or sister has gone to bed. Even if parents are tired or have lots to do, they enjoy this as much as their children.

If your brother or sister goes away sometimes for respite care, you might feel relieved to have time alone with your Mum or Dad. But you might also miss them and feel guilty about them going away. Parents often feel confused too, so it's a good chance to talk about your feelings.

It's OK to be angry sometimes

Sometimes you may feel that there's no one to talk to, or no one else in your position. But, in fact, there are thousands of children in the same boat. Like you, they sometimes feel angry and upset about their brother or sister with disability, even though they love them and enjoy spending lots of time with them.

It is best to talk about your feelings, either to your Mum or Dad, or another adult you know. They will try to help you understand why you sometimes feel upset or angry.

Ask your Mum or Dad to explain your brother's or sister's disability and what you can do to help. Remember it is not your fault! You are important and special too!

My brother or sister always wants to play with us

If you can include your brother or sister in your games in even a small way, that's great. But sometimes you won't want to. You have your needs too, and it's OK if you want to play just with your friends or be by yourself sometimes. Make sure your parents know you want to do this. They will understand that you sometimes get frustrated by your brother or sister.

Sometimes I get teased

Everyone does care what other people think of them. You might feel uncomfortable because most families don't have a child with disability, or maybe friends at school stare or tease.

Try and talk with some other children in the same position and find out how they cope with the same feelings – perhaps you could meet some through your brother's or sister's special school.

Tell your Mum or Dad – or a teacher – if you are being teased or bullied. Don't try to cope with it alone and don't try to pretend you don't mind if you do.

Remember that people usually tease only because they simply don't understand about disability.

What will happen in the future?

Children who have brothers or sisters with disabilities sometimes feel very worried about the future. They ask themselves many questions like these:

Who will look after my brother or sister? Will my brother or sister die? Will I have a disabled child myself?

If you do worry about the future, talk

to someone and ask advice. Even if Mum or Dad is tired or busy, say that you're worried and that you'd like to discuss something with them.

Sometimes I can't talk to Mum or Dad

Children can sometimes find talking to their parents about how they are feeling very difficult. So why not talk to someone outside your immediate family – perhaps an aunt or uncle, or a family friend or perhaps a teacher at your school? Sometimes it's nice to talk to someone who's less involved, who will take you seriously and keep your chat confidential.

Tips for parents

Parents bringing up a child with disabilities at home do an incredible job, often with little help. This article will provide a starting-point for you and your other children to talk about some of the issues which affect the family.

When do I tell my other children?

The realisation that your child has a disability is distressing and difficult. Apart from your own concern, your other children may start to feel left out, anxious, frightened or guilty.

Tell them about their brother's or sister's disability as soon as possible. Make sure they understand that it does not threaten them and that they are not responsible. Explain how worried you are, but also try to be positive about the child's special needs.

I worry I don't spend enough time with my other children

Caring for a child with disabilities can be a full-time job to parents, and you may find yourself giving a disproportionate amount of time to that child. As a result, your other children may sometimes feel resentful.

Make a point of telling them how special they are too. Set time aside to spend alone with your other children to talk about their special interests. Feelings of love, anger and frustration can be confusing for children, and they may bottle up resentment in order to protect Mum or Dad. Encourage them to talk about these difficult emotions and let them know it is alright to feel angry or upset.

Age	10-11	12-13	14-15	Total
Boys				
No disability	95	95	94	95
Moderate disability	4	4	5	4
Serious disability	1	1	0	1
Girls				
No disability	97	95	92	95
Moderate disability	3	5	7	5
Serious disability	1	0	1	1

Prevalence of disability among children
Ages 10-15 years old, 1995 (%)

Source: Health Survey for England 1995. SCPR on behalf of the DoH, 1997

Explain why their brother or sister with a disability is taking up a good deal of your time, and thank them for their help and patience.

Playing together

Play time is as important for children with disabilities as anyone else, and if their brothers or sisters can include them it is rewarding for everyone. Even watching can be fun if the child is actively included.

However, your children may still feel frustrated when a sibling with disabilities disrupts their games with other friends – it is difficult to accommodate a child's special needs at all times. Let your children know they are entitled to time for themselves and that it is not something they need feel guilty about.

I don't want the other children to feel embarrassed

The public is often very intolerant of disability. Being stared at in public, called names, or teased can be incredibly painful for a child. There is no easy answer to intolerance and prejudice, but encourage your children to talk to you about these problems and together work out positive ways to deal with the public's reaction to their brother or sister.

The other children worry about the future

The brothers and sisters of children with disabilities often take on many emotional and practical responsibilities. As they grow older, they may feel they should be looking after their sibling and not doing what they would rather do. It is important to

support them in leading their own lives and leaving home.

Older children can be concerned that they too could have a child with disability – your GP or consultant should be able to provide information.

Is there anyone out there like us?

Feeling isolated is one of the biggest problems for children who have a brother or sister with a disability. Meeting others in the same position – through the school of your child with disability, for example – provides a chance to share experiences and find support.

Encourage your children to talk to other adults who are less involved – relatives or family friends.

Is respite care for us?

If respite care is available in your area, it provides an invaluable chance to spend time with your other children – as well as giving the parents themselves a much needed break!

Make sure you are confident about the care your child with disabilities will receive and ask if the whole family can see the respite centre and meet the staff.

Don't feel guilty about wanting a break – make the most of it! Respite care breaks are good for you, good for your child with disability and good for your other children.

• NCH Action for Children helps many thousands of Britain's most vulnerable children towards a better life through over 230 projects nationwide

© NCH Action for Children

Unequal opportunities

Children with disabilities and their families speak out

'Other children have the right to go to school, go out to play, go to the pictures on Saturday mornings, to have a shower or go to the loo when they want. My child has to wait for someone to take her, for a suitable loo to be there when she wants it. All the basic choices are denied her – and people seem to think it quite outrageous when I want the same things for her which her sister takes for granted.'

'We feel like we are always fighting for things, and sometimes it's hard enough just getting by day to day without having to fight for things.'

'If there was more interaction in schools or some form of teaching, perhaps the children of today could grow up knowing that people with special needs were people who need care and understanding and not someone to make fun of.'

Introduction

Unequal Opportunities – children with disabilities and their families speak out reports the findings of NCH Action for Children research concerning the lives of children with disabilities living in the community, and of their families, following recent major legislative and financial change. NCH Action for Children's commissioning of this research in our 125th anniversary year underlines our continuing commitment to providing high quality services to these children and families, and to advocating both with them and on their behalf.

This study demonstrates just how unequal are the opportunities for children with disabilities and their families in Britain today. We hope that its publication will help achieve two very important, linked objectives:

1. To encourage public acceptance of the notion that children and adults with disabilities have a right to extra help so that they

are able to fulfil their potential as citizens in our society.
2. To persuade government to direct more resources to children and adults with disabilities, so that their needs can be met.

The research

The findings are based on the views of 83 carers of children with disabilities living at home – most of them mothers, but including some fathers, grandparents and foster carers. These were gathered through a written questionnaire distributed via nineteen of NCH Action for Children's community-based projects for children with disabilities, across Britain.

The study was also informed by eighteen in-depth interviews with

parents; by group interviews with a number of children with disabilities; with a support group for siblings; and by discussions with staff working in NCH Action for Children projects.

4 in 5 of respondents to the written questionnaire had a child with severe or very severe disabilities. 1 in 8 also had another member of the household with a serious health problem. 1 in 5 were lone parents and nearly 1 in 3 had three or more children living with them.

Key findings

Three important themes emerged from the study, concerning services, finances and attitudes.

1: Services

• There are too few support services for children with disabilities – especially those which are preventive – and because of scarce resources families have to fight to gain access to them.

'It is one long battle for this and that. Why do you have to be at the end of your tether before any help is forthcoming?' (mother of a girl aged 19 with learning difficulties)

- But both parents and children reported the crucial role which support services play in keeping families together.

'I liked it (respite care) from the beginning – it was a break, …I felt like the only one, but since I went there I realised I wasn't the only one, there are children there with all sorts of problems.' (girl aged 11 with a progressive muscular disease)

- Even within this 'elite sample' of families already in touch with helping agencies, 2 in 5 thought there was a need for more respite care. More speech therapy, physiotherapy and comprehensive domiciliary services are also required.
- Respondents thought local authorities could do more to put into practice the principle in the Children Act 1989 of working in partnership with parents and carers.

'Please discuss services with parents/carers before setting them up. Lip service is no good to us.' (mother of a 10-year-old boy with Down's syndrome and chronic juvenile rheumatoid arthritis)

- 3 in 4 respondents thought there was insufficient information published locally about those services which are available. Families of other children with disabilities are often the best information source, which means that isolated families lose out.

2: Finances

- Nearly 2 in 3 said they were not managing well financially. During the last year 2 in 3 had drawn on savings; nearly half had borrowed to meet a big expense and 1 in 5 had borrowed just to get by.
- More than 4 in 5 had extra costs because of their child's disability and of these, 4 in 5 said that these extra costs were not met in full by benefits.

'I spend extra on clothes – maybe £250 a year? – and he's bigger now. Because he bites coats, breaks the zips and buttons and scuffs his shoes.' (mother of a boy with autism)

- 1 in 10 had gone into debt because of the extra costs due to their

Children with disability

Great Britain 1985. Per '000	Aged 0-4	Aged 5-9	Aged 10-15
Locomotion	5	10	11
Reaching and stretching	2	2	2
Dexterity	2	4	4
Seeing	2	2	2
Hearing	3	8	6
Personal care	6	10	6
Continence	6	14	8
Communication	5	13	13
Behaviour	13	23	24
Intellectual functioning	4	9	11
Consciousness	5	5	4
Eating, drinking, digestion	1	1	–
Disfigurement	1	1	2

Source: OPCS Survey of Disability GB 1989

child's disability and nearly 1 in 10 (1 in 4 of lone parents) said they couldn't meet these extra costs.

- More than 3 in 4 thought there was insufficient, simple information available about the benefits to which they might be entitled.
- In theory many families are entitled to help from health and local authorities with capital expenditure required by their child's disability. In practice, because of budget constraints or delays, too many end up buying these expensive goods themselves.

'I said to the supervisor "What about the stairs?" (up to the front door) and she said "Don't worry, you'll get a ramp." And it took twelve years!' (mother of a 13-year-old boy with cerebral palsy and epilepsy)

- Many families find the assessment forms they are required to complete in order to apply for grants and benefits are overly intrusive, and some choose not to do so and so forego help which should rightfully be theirs.

3: Attitudes

- This study shows that public attitudes in Britain towards children with disabilities and their families remain, in too many cases, discriminatory:

'they all get into little gangs and bully me… I just run away and find my Mum.' (child with learning difficulties)

'I've had old friends see me when I was out walking her when she was a

baby and they've crossed the road to avoid me, they're so embarrassed.' (mother of a girl aged 11 with global retardation)

- More than 9 in 10 said that they worried about the future for their children with disabilities and three-quarters of all lone parents said that they worried a great deal.

Their concerns are due to several factors:

1. A feeling that society fails to understand, and therefore meet the needs of people with disabilities.

'People with disabilities need to be seen as valuable members of society who have rights the same as the rest of us, and a great deal to offer.' (mother of a 6-year-old boy with Down's syndrome)

2. A fear that services that presently exist may be eroded by spending cuts.

3. Awareness of the present chronic shortages of independent, supported housing for people with disabilities; of employment and training opportunities; and of 'transition to adulthood' support services for young disabled people.

4. Profound concern about who will advocate on behalf of their child once they are gone:

'I don't know about the future of my child and what happens after me… Other children can stand on their own feet. But these can't speak for their rights – they need someone to fight for them.' (mother of a 19-year-old young man with cerebral palsy)

© NCH Action for Children

No way out

There is one group of Londoners with little to celebrate, denied access to the sights and nights of the 'world's coolest city' because they happen to be disabled. By Tony Thompson

It is a well-known fact that young, disabled people lead sad little lives. They have no interest in live music, don't care much for the theatre or comedy and feel no need to catch up with the latest releases at the cinema. Furthermore they don't like to socialise down the pub with their mates and they rarely eat out, probably because they prefer to cook for themselves. Oh, and young disabled people – all of whom have to use wheelchairs, regardless of the nature of their disability – are not trendy. After all, you never see them at any of the trendy places so they simply can't be.

This, it seems, is what the owners and managers of London's top pubs, clubs and cinemas believe, according to a new survey conducted by Artsline, the information and advice service for disabled users of arts and entertainment venues. When asked for a reason behind the low number of disabled people passing through their doors, the majority cited a 'lack of interest' in whatever they had to offer. But rather like the age-old joke that cottage cheese must make you fat because you only ever see fat people eating it, London's venues are simply failing to see the whole picture.

'It seems to me that young disabled people are not supposed to go to the "in" places,' says one teenage wheelchair user. 'There are some people who are willing to go out there and do it anyway, but they have to put up with a lot of flak and have really thick skins. I don't see why anyone should have to subject themselves to that simply to have a night out. That's the reason most people end up staying in. It's a vicious circle. Because they never see other disabled people out enjoying themselves, they don't realise they can.'

> **'I had to give my wheelchair to the staff and they took it away somewhere for safekeeping. But when the film finished, the staff had gone home and forgotten to give me my chair back'**

According to Artsline, there could be as many as 490,000 disabled Londoners between the ages of 14 and 25. Almost every one will have a horror story about being denied access to something or somewhere because of their disability. Artsline's survey found that music venues and clubs have the worst reputation, with just 40 per cent of those in London being fully accessible. Complaints of poor door policies are also common. One wheelchair user and regular club-goer was recently denied entry to one south London venue. The door staff repeatedly asked her whether she had been to anything like it before and even when she confirmed that she had they refused to let her in, insisting that it 'simply isn't your kind of thing'.

The situation is little better when it comes to cinemas. Just 43 per cent of those in the capital are accessible. The Odeon West End was refurbished in 1994, but it is only possible for wheelchair users to use the cinema if they are able to get up the stairs and into one of the seats. 'My wheelchair is part of me', says Adam. 'Asking me to leave it is just like asking someone to take off their trousers before they go in to see the film.'

'One time, I went to the late show at the Empire. I had to give my wheelchair to the staff and they took it away somewhere for safekeeping.

But when the film finished, the staff had gone home and forgotten to give me my chair back.'

When it comes to fringe cinemas, the figure for accessibility rises to a respectable 76 per cent, but Artsline says this is because such cinemas are often based in community halls and other venues that regularly cater to the disabled. Other smaller cinemas have taken advantage of lottery money to expand and made themselves fully accessible in the process.

Visiting Theatreland is yet another problem. Although 58 per cent claim to be accessible, this often applies only to seats with restricted views or to boxes, which cost up to £80 and are well beyond the reach of anyone trying to get by on benefits.

The venues contacted in the Artsline survey said that, on average, they saw one to five disabled people every two weeks, but all referred to disabled people as wheelchair users – invisible disabilities such as deafness were not included and generally even less well catered for.

And those disabled people who do venture out have already had to overcome a number of obstacles. Transport is perhaps top of the list. Of 273 Underground stations in the capital, 40 are designated as being wheelchair friendly. But, in reality, this tends to apply only to one platform or one part of the station, making it completely useless for anyone trying to make a return journey. Only 13 stations are fully accessible so unless your venue happens to be alongside one of them, the Underground is out.

A spokeswoman for Artsline told *Time Out*: 'Lack of enthusiasm is definitely not the reason why young disabled people are not going out. Obviously, lack of access is a major problem but it is also complicated by other factors and an inaccessible transport system makes it impossible for a young disabled person to afford to pay for taxi fares and an entrance fee, especially if they live outside central London. Some parents are naturally overprotective, but this could be because they are not fully aware of facilities. When a disabled person has access to information about a venue, it allows them to make an informed choice about where they can go.'

During the Labour Party conference, a three-point plan to improve the civil rights of disabled people was announced. Andrew Smith, minister responsible for Equal Opportunities, told delegates in Brighton that he would create a ministerial taskforce to recommend the way forward on the issue. He also pledged to set up a Disability Rights Commission, to 'enforce, advise and promote good practice'.

But two weeks ago, the Government admitted that plans were being made to cut social security benefits for Britain's 6.5 million disabled people – a move that would leave even less cash in the pockets of the young people who are already struggling to get by.

Spending on disability benefits has soared from £4.1 billion in 1982 to £23.5bn last year. The new Government proposals aim not just to stop the rise but actually to reverse it, a suggestion that has led to outrage among charities dealing with the disabled.

Last month, Ian Malcolm-Walker, co-vice chair of the Labour Party Disabled Members' Group, wrote to Baroness Hollis, junior social security minister responsible for disability benefits at the DSS: 'We now say publicly and very clearly that the very support and trust of the disabled people that helped Labour so much on May 1 is at risk. Removing or altering the entitlement is not the answer.'

© *Time Out*
December, 1997

Fight on the home front

Diary of a parent with a disabled child. Sarah Davies on a bizarre means test that is depriving her of a grant to adapt her house to meet her daughter's needs

We were a very ordinary sort of family once, until the birth of our third child, Sarah, changed our lives for ever and we came to learn of the Treasury concept of 'excess income'.

We are teachers. We met at university, fell in love, married, bought a house and had two children. The house is a three-bedroom semi bought in 1991 for £76,000. The mortgage of £297 a month, taken on in the expectation that I would return to work, is our largest single outgoing.

We paid our bills, bought food and clothes and the occasional treat and, like thousands of others, lived just about within our means.

Every item your child needs has to be fought for through a barrage of forms

Sarah was born in 1992, with severe cerebral palsy. She also has epilepsy and is profoundly deaf. It is probably not possible to convey what it is like to discover that your child is severely disabled. You are left on your own to cope. Every item your child needs has to be fought for through a barrage of forms demanding proof of the level of disability and the degree of your poverty. Now Sarah is five, we get the full component of Disability Living Allowance: £84.10 per week.

Does this seem a lot? When you have a disabled child, you soon learn it goes nowhere. Government research shows that if you are a parent of one of Britain's 150,000 disabled children, you will be 16 per cent poorer than you would otherwise have been and face greater risk of break-up within the family. There is also an 80 per cent chance that the housing you have is not suitable.

Housing was a major problem for us. Carrying Sarah was a strain on our backs, and our toilet is upstairs. Even more desperate was the lack of space. A child in a wheelchair needs room to move around, but our living room had also to accommodate the bulky equipment she has to have. We needed to move or to extend our house: we could not afford either.

We applied to the council for a disabled facilities grant (DFG), which exists to give disabled people access to normal facilities in their home. Their occupational therapist specified a downstairs extension to provide a ground-floor bedroom and en suite facilities for Sarah. The grants officer told us the work would cost £28,000, but warned us of a means test prescribed by the Treasury that councils cannot vary.

We were not worried. I had given up work to care for Sarah. All our costs – heating, laundry, transport and telephone – had gone up. When they saw our incomings and out-goings our need would be obvious. The officer asked about our income. Then he said that, according to the Treasury formula, we had 'excess income' of £182.11 a week, enough to borrow £14,802. Unless we paid this in full we would get no help. We were dumbfounded: our income was stretched to the limit. He had not asked about our mortgage costs; wasn't this a mistake?

There was no mistake. This is a means test which calculates what a family can afford without considering outgoings. The calculation is a fantasy, but to the thousands of families it affects it is a nightmare.

What has the consequence been? It is two years since the occupational therapist told us what our child needed, but we have no hope of getting it. Sarah has no space to play and no proper facilities for

If you are a parent of one of Britain's 150,000 disabled children, you will be 16 per cent poorer than you would otherwise have been and face greater risk of break-up within the family

independence and dignity. What are we to do? If we sold our house and applied for rented accommodation, we would be treated as intentionally homeless.

All over the country there are others whose children are suffering because of this savage and unrealistic rule. A group called Homes Fit for Children has been formed to fight for a fair means test. Yesterday it met the All Party Disablement Group to ask how MPs can help.

For us, there has been a final blow. We thought that if my husband could earn more money we might, after all, be able to borrow the £14,802. He got an increment and we contacted the council. We have just learned that because his salary has gone up (it is now £25,899) his contribution to the work our daughter needs has been reassessed – at £23,000.

Disabled groups protest at 'inadequate' legislation

By David Brindle, Social Services Correspondent

Disabled people's groups are protesting at what they say is the inadequacy of the Disability Discrimination Act, the first main provisions of which come into force today.

Rights Now, a coalition of 64 groups, is organising a lobby of MPs at Westminster to call for a toughening of the act and a new civil rights bill for the 6.5 million disabled people in the UK.

From today it will be unlawful to refuse service to a disabled person or provide an inferior service. A hotel pretending it was fully booked to keep out a person with a learning disability, or a severe disfigurement, could be sued in the courts.

It will also be unlawful for larger employers, defined as those with more than 20 staff, to discriminate against disabled workers or job applicants. Employers covered by the act will be required to make 'reasonable adjustments' to meet the needs of disabled staff. Breach of any of the act's employment provisions could be challenged at an industrial tribunal.

Most disability groups are angry that further provisions of the act, affecting access to buildings and public transport, may not come into force for nine years.

There is also resentment that an advisory council, not a statutory commission, has been set up to monitor the act and that the legislation does permit discrimination in certain circumstances – such as on health and safety grounds.

Stephen Bradshaw, chairman of Rights Now, said: 'We want an act with teeth, not this harmful and discriminatory law. Proper civil rights legislation would unlock the potential of millions of disabled people.'

However, David Grayson, chairman of the advisory body on the act, the National Disability Council, said that today was a 'red-letter day' for disabled people because the new law would have far-reaching effects.

The man who would kill disabled babies

World expert on medical ethics is condemned by doctors for saying that new-born children with severe disabilities should have their lives ended by lethal injection. By Jeremy Laurance, Health Editor

Doctors' leaders yesterday condemned an expert on medical ethics who called for babies with severe disabilities to be given lethal injections to end their lives.

Professor Peter Singer, deputy director of the Centre for Human Bioethics at Monash University in Australia, said that in cases where doctors and parents agreed that a baby's disabilities were so overwhelming as to be incompatible with a decent quality of life, it would be kinder to end the baby's life deliberately rather than leave it to die.

'The standard practice is to withhold treatment such as antibiotics or in some cases feeding so the babies do die either from untreated infections or from starvation and dehydration,' he said on BBC Radio 4's *Today* programme.

'I think that is cruel and inhumane. It causes unnecessary suffering to the infants and their families. Once you make a decision that it is better that the baby dies you ought to be able to make sure that it dies easily and swiftly. That means by giving it a lethal injection.'

The Royal College of Paediatrics and Child Health said that although there were cases in which it might be appropriate to withhold or withdraw treatment there was no justification for killing children. Guidelines on when to withhold or withdraw treatment were issued by the college last year.

Professor Richard Cook, consultant neo-natalogist and spokesman for the college, said: 'What I feel about people who want to bump patients off is that they are doing it for themselves. It is very difficult for doctors faced with patients for whom they can do nothing surrounded by parents and nurses who are distressed. The easiest thing is to bump them off. I don't think that is the right thing to do.'

He was 'concerned for the needless suffering which exists now, as a result of current practice'

The guidelines specify five situations in which it may be right to withdraw treatment, if the doctors, nurses and parents agree. They include a child who is brain dead, a child who has no chance of survival and for whom treatment may prolong their suffering and one who may survive but who would be so impaired that treatment would in effect add to their suffering.

The British Medical Association said there was a key ethical distinction between killing and leaving a patient to die that lay at the heart of a doctor's duty to their patients. Dr Bill O'Neill, its science and ethics adviser, said: 'There is a very important difference between withholding treatment and deliberately doing something to end a patient's life. Patients are not just left to die – all efforts are made to ensure they are comfortable and they do not suffer.'

Professor Singer, who is in the UK to give a series of seminars, was challenged on the *Today* programme by Jacqueline Lang, a lawyer and author of *Human Lives*. She said: 'We can eradicate suffering by eradicating the sufferer. It matters how we get good results. We cannot use any means to achieve an end, however good that end might be.'

But he said he was 'concerned for the needless suffering which exists now, as a result of current practice'.

© The Independent
May, 1998

Social inclusion

Making it happen. Information from Disability Daily

Social inclusion means . . .
Being treated as valued members of society, having the same rights and responsibilities as non-disabled people and being able to fully participate at every level of society.

To have a real social inclusion the UK's 8.5 million disabled people would need:

- to live in their own, accessible homes within their local communities.
- to get around safely and confidently with fully accessible public transport and to be free from harassment.
- to have equal access to employment and real career options
- to enjoy the same leisure opportunities (sport, shopping, cinema) as non-disabled people.
- to live free from poverty with help towards the extra costs of disability as of right

but . . . the reality of being disabled in Britain is very different
Inaccessible housing and public transport, employment discrimination, inadequate disability benefits: all these things push disabled people to the margins of society and tell them they don't belong.

The situation is much worse for black and ethnic minority disabled people who experience double discrimination:

- Over 80% of people with reduced mobility live in inaccessible homes.
- Four out of five disabled people have problems with transport and two-thirds say difficulty using public transport is one reason for not going out more.
- Raising a severely disabled child cost three times as much as a non-disabled child.
- Disabled people are more than twice as likely to be unemployed as non-disabled people.
- 65% of disabled people live in or on the margins of poverty.

and carers face social exclusion too . . .

- One in six adults in the UK is a carer.
- Carers save the state £34 billion per year yet many do not get any benefits or support services.
- The main carers' benefit Invalid Care Allowance is one of the lowest of its kind worth less than 11% of average earnings.
- Carers over 65 are among the poorest in society and the vast majority are not entitled to Invalid Care Allowance. The majority of these carers are women.
- One in five carers has never had a break. This makes it hard to do things which other people take for granted like seeing a film or visiting relatives.

. . . so . . . what can be done?
If society is to include disabled people and carers as full and equal members we are going to have to make a lot of changes – changes which will not only benefit disabled people but will enrich us as a society. We can all make a difference.

There are simple things everyone can do to include disabled people . . .

- We can keep pavements and corridors free of clutter.
- We can learn new ways to communicate.
- We can provide information in accessible formats.
- We can look at people's abilities as well as their disabilities.
- We can stop making assumptions, and consult with disabled people on their own terms.
- We can respect difference and challenge stereotyped media coverage of disabled people.
- We can challenge policies and practices where we work, shop and live which deny equal access to disabled people.

. . . sometimes it's simply a question of making sure a disabled person or carer gets what they are entitled to . . .
Disabled people can get legal redress if they are denied proper support services to enable them to live independently, but too few understand their rights or know where to go for help.

If a local authority doesn't provide transport for someone to attend a local college, for example, there may be other agencies which can help.

Under the Carers Act 1995, carers are entitled to have their own needs assessed and for those needs to be taken into consideration in the provision of services.

Providers of goods and services are no longer allowed to offer disabled people a less favourable service but many are not aware of their legal obligations.

Many employers are not aware of the Access to Work scheme (which can provide technical and financial support to disabled people seeking work or in work) or of simple cost-effective steps to support carers in work

. . . but . . . we need Government action to make social inclusion a reality for all disabled people and carers . . .

- If more resources were invested in personal assistance services and technical aids, with each person entitled to national minimum standards of community care, independent living could become a reality for all.
- If tough action was taken on inaccessible transport disabled people could enjoy real mobility and freedom.
- If rights to advocacy were strengthened more disabled people could take real control of their lives.

- If every disabled person had access to employment opportunities and workplace support the economy would benefit from an influx of new skills and we'd all be better off as a society.
- If the benefits system was based on entitlement, not grudging hand-outs, and tailored to individual needs disabled people would have higher status in society and lead less stressful lives.
- If disability benefits were reformed to create a more level playing field between disabled and non-disabled people, we would be a more inclusive society.
- If carers had rights to short-term breaks as of right, an adequate carers' allowance and a proper pension they too would feel more valued by society and more able to play a full part in it.

so . . . what is the Government doing?
The Government has pledged:
- to strengthen civil rights in employ-ment, transport, access to goods and services and education
- to disability benefits to provide opportunity for those who can work, and security for those who can't
- to examine the creation of a Citizen-ship Pension for carers who are outside the labour market
- to take action to tackle the stigma and discrimination faced by people with mental health problems.

It has already . . .
- introduced measures to make it easier to move off benefits into work
- invested in creating new job opportunities for disabled people
- changed the building regulation so that new houses will be more accessible to disabled people.

It's a good start but it is only a start
Please join us in Disability Daily to make social inclusion for disabled people happen.

© Disability Daily
July, 1998

Children with a disability

The most recent and comprehensive survey of the prevalence of disabilities in children was carried out by the OPCS in 1985 and 1988, and published in 1989. It estimated that there were some 360,000 children aged 16 and under with a disability in the UK. Of these, 2% (about 5,600) lived in some sort of communal establishment (compared to 7% of disabled adults). The majority of children (nearly two-thirds) had more than one type of disability.

The survey showed that:
- 3 per cent of all children under 16 have a disability;
- 4.5 per cent of boys and 3 per cent of girls between 5-9 were affected;
- children over 5 were more likely to have a disability. (This may be in part due to the greater identification of disabilities once a child starts school.);
- behavioural disabilities were the most common form of disability, followed by disabilities in the area of communication, locomotion and continence;

- North Yorkshire, Humberside, East Anglia and the South East (excluding London) had the highest rate of disability;
- West Midlands and the South West had the lowest rates of disability;
- the majority of children with disabilities in Britain live in the community.

The OPCS (now the Office for National Statistics) survey attempted to quantify the severity of disability. This was achieved by taking into account the type of each individual's disability or combination of disabilities and the extent to which these limited the performance of daily activities. Individuals were ranked 1 to 10, 1 being the lowest 10 being the most severe.

The definition of disability used by these two studies was that used by the World Health Organisation, i.e. 'A restriction or lack of ability to perform normal activities which has resulted from impairment of a structure or function of body and mind'. This definition is based on a medical notion of disability, defining it as being similar to an illness and as a functional limitation. It has been strongly criticised and organisations of disabled people have argued that by conceptualising disability as an individual rather than a societal problem, solutions have been sought in the individual sphere, for example through therapy and technical or personal support. However, it is increasingly clear that the individual abilities of disabled people very much depend on attitudinal, architectural and structural barriers of the environment, and on the willingness of society to include or exclude the needs of disabled people.

Published in 1997, the Health Survey for England 1995 contained questions on disability which were asked of children aged 10 to 15. Overall the Health Survey for England 1995 found that around 5 per cent of girls and boys had at least one disability, with 1 per cent having a serious disability. These findings are broadly consistent with, although slightly higher than, the 1985 OPCS study.

© NCH Factfile

Disability

Key facts and guidance for managers

Definition

There are three broad categories of disability:

- sensory impairment

- physical impairment

- learning disability

- The Government's definition [Disability Discrimination Act 1995] provides that someone has a disability if they have a physical or mental impairment which has a long-term adverse effect on their ability to carry out normal day-to-day activities.
- To be long term, the effect must have lasted for, or be expected to last, for 12 months.
- Disabilities cover mobility; manual dexterity; physical co-ordination; continence; ability to lift, carry or move everyday objects; speech, hearing or eyesight; memory or ability to learn or understand; or perception of danger risk.
- In addition, certain degenerative diseases such as cancer and ME, being HIV positive or suffering facial disfigurement, are also covered by the Act.

Background

In the past there have been rudimentary employment services for registered disabled people, such as supported employment schemes, assisted fares to work and job introduction grants to employers.

- Under the Disabled Persons [Employment] Acts, employers [unless exempt] were supposed to maintain a quota of 3 per cent registered disabled people.
- Pressure to legislate to prevent discrimination – in employment, in access to goods and services, in transport and in education – against people with disabilities had been mounting in the UK, particularly since the passing of

Information from the Industrial Society

the Americans With Disabilities Act [ADA] in the USA in 1990.

Key facts

It is estimated that there are about 6.2 million disabled people in the UK. Fewer than 5 per cent use wheelchairs. 2.4 million disabled people are of working age, but of these only 35 per cent are in work.

- Of those who become disabled while in employment, only 25 per cent are in work 12 months later.
- Some 1 in 4 customers are disabled or close to a disabled person in their family. So there is a strong business argument for organisations to make provision for disabled people, whether as employees, customers or users of their services.
- Discrimination against disabled people is a result of cultural, attitudinal and environmental barriers – for example any suggestion of past mental illness can give rise to discrimination.
- All of us will experience some form of disability or impairment some time in our lives. However, many disabilities are cyclical, many last for a limited period and many have only a limited effect.
- Research into people's attitudes shows that 92 per cent of us feel admiration, 74 per cent pity, 58 per cent embarrassment and 41 per cent fear when confronted with disability. This explains why people have been unwilling to register as disabled, believing it to be a disadvantage. The task of changing attitudes is a major, long-term challenge.

State of play

Employers are concerned about the potential costs of compliance with legislation, whereas groups representing disabled people argue that the legislation may not go far enough either in guaranteeing access to goods, services and facilities or in powers of enforcement.

Following lobbying by various disability groups, the Disability Discrimination Act 1995 now provides similar protection to that in the Sex Discrimination and Race Relations Acts.

But there is one major difference. The National Disability Council – unlike the Equal Opportunities Commission or the Commission for Racial Equality – will have advisory powers only, but no statutory powers of enforcement.

The new Act sets out:

- a statutory right of non-discrimination in employment;

- the elimination of potential discrimination in financial services;

- creation of the National Disability Council with an advisory role, and responsibility for drawing up Codes of Practice;

- improved access to public transport;

- improved access standards for schools.

The Act comes into effect in 1996.

Best practice guidelines

The Industrial Society has always advocated a positive approach, concentrating on what people can, rather than what they cannot do.

- We recommend that organisations should draw up plans with short, medium and longer-term objectives for improvement to employment practices, access and service provision.

- Disability awareness is vital, and organisations should provide relevant training, advice and information to all employees.
- Problems are more likely to arise in changing employees' attitudes to customers and colleagues, rather than in adapting premises and providing equipment.
- If people with disabilities can't work for you, you miss out on the skills, abilities and creativity of diverse teams, and you are giving the wrong message to existing and potential customers.
- Many improvements to premises are low [or no] cost and can be included in existing maintenance or refurbishment programmes.
- Improved access to, and movement within, premises supports good health and safety practice anyway, and improves the quality of working life for everyone.
- Draw up an action plan, with priorities and time scales.
- Train staff in disability awareness.

Industrial Society help

The Industrial Society training pack, *Equal Opportunities*, is designed to help raise awareness of prejudices, discrimination and stereotypes, not only in cases of sex and race discrimination, but also discrimination against disability.

- Industrial Society courses on dealing with discrimination, creating a positive work environment, equal opportunities, and managing diversity are all available in-house, adapted to organisations' particular needs.

- The Industrial Society Information Service has copies of organisations' policies on disability.

- The Society's *Managing Best Practice* No 14 on Managing Diversity covers disability employment issues.

- For further information please contact: The Industrial Society Information Service on 0171 262 2401. The address details can be found on page 41 of this book.

© The Industrial Society
January, 1998

Study shows disabled prejudice

By David Brindle, Social Services Correspondent

Disabled people remain victims of widespread prejudice and discrimination that often make them feel outcasts, according to research published today by a leading disability charity.

The Government risks ignoring problems faced by disabled people by drawing too narrow a definition of 'social exclusion', says the charity, Leonard Cheshire.

The research is based on an NOP telephone survey of 1,000 people, more than half of whom had no regular contact with anybody with a disability. More than one in five admitted feeling awkward or self-conscious in the presence of a disabled person.

Almost one in three agreed with a statement that 'some people assume that a person in a wheelchair cannot be intelligent'. A similar proportion said disabled people should not expect to be able to use public transport.

More than 40 per cent felt it was 'virtually impossible' for disabled people to get a job and almost three in four thought that their standard of living would fall if they became disabled.

The findings are supported by comments by disabled people who took part in focus group discussions organised by the charity. One said: 'Since I've become ill, all my friends have disappeared. People don't want to know.'

Others reported being targets of mockery with gangs of young people said to be the worst offenders.

Leonard Cheshire, which is celebrating its golden jubilee, is today launching an advertising campaign on the theme of 'enabling' disabled people. The charity wants ministers to incorporate disability fully within the work of its social exclusion unit.

It says: 'By limiting social exclusion to the effects of extreme poverty, the Government ignores a whole area which disabled people – not to mention a whole lot of other groups – know only too well: that of being excluded from society because of the attitudes of others.'

© The Guardian
June, 1998

What is a learning disability?

Information from Mencap

Around one child in 100 is born with a learning disability, or develops a learning disability while they are very young.

A child with a learning disability will probably learn more slowly than other children of the same age, but it is wrong to think that all people with learning disabilities are the same.

In fact, every person with a learning disability is different – with different abilities, interests, likes and dislikes. Just like everyone else!

Do children with learning disabilities learn more slowly than other children?

Everybody learns at different speeds. Some children will learn quickly and others will learn more slowly.

Someone with a learning disability will learn much more slowly than you. They may not be able to spell, read, write or draw as well as you. They might also find it harder to understand questions, or be less able at ordinary things like dressing or catching a bus home.

Some people with a learning disability can learn to do these things, but it will probably take a little longer.

Don't forget, there may also be things that someone with a learning disability can do better than you, like painting, drawing, dance, music or sport.

Why do people with learning disabilities sometimes behave differently?

People with learning disabilities sometimes behave in ways which seem unusual. For example, someone with a learning disability may make more noise in the classroom than you do. Or they may move their head or body unexpectedly.

mencap

Some people with a learning disability will also find it harder to talk clearly. This is because they have a physical disability which affects their speech. Someone with Down's Syndrome, for example, will have a longer tongue than average. This means their tongue will sometimes hang outside their mouth, and make it harder to talk. Try talking with your tongue outside your mouth and see for yourself!

People with learning disabilities sometimes behave differently because they may think in younger ways than other children. But it is important to remember their real age, and not to 'baby' them. You can help by showing them the way you behave. Then they can learn from you. At other times you may learn from them.

Do children with a learning disability go to school?

Yes. All children with learning disabilities go to school, often until they are 19 years old. Many children with learning disabilities go to ordinary 'mainstream' schools, like yours.

Some mainstream schools have a separate class for children with special educational needs. Other schools put an extra teacher or assistant in an ordinary class, to help those pupils with learning disabilities.

How are special schools different from mainstream schools?

Some children with learning disabilities go to a special school, where they can get extra help.

There are many similarities be=tween mainstream and special schools. A special school has teachers, lessons and playtime too. But there are also differences. In a special school there are fewer pupils in each class (maybe around ten). Some special schools have other staff to help too, like physiotherapists who help children to develop movement skills.

Children who have a learning disability may need more help with basic language and number skills, rather than learning separate subjects, like French, history or geography.

A special school may also teach children how to be more independent, so that they can dress and wash themselves, do simple cooking, and look after themselves with less help. You probably learned these things very easily, but if someone has a learning disability it can take a great deal of hard work.

Is learning disability very common?

Learning disability is the most common disability there is. You may already know someone with a learning disability, either in your school or neighbourhood, or a friend or relative.

Over one million people in Britain have some form of learning disability, including over 190,000 adults and children with a severe learning disability. So it is important to understand a little about it, and how it affects people's lives.

Is learning disability the same as mental illness?

No. Learning disability is not the same as mental illness. If you are born with a learning disability, or develop one while you are very young, you will always have a learning disability, although the effects of a learning disability can be lessened with special help and education. Learning disability is not an illness and cannot be cured.

What other kinds of disability are there?

Learning disability is the most common disability, but there are other kinds of disability too.

A physical disability affects movements. Someone with a physical disability may have more difficulty walking or controlling their arms. They may also find it hard to speak clearly because their mouth may be affected too.

Someone with a sensory disability will have extra difficulty seeing or hearing. The extra difficulty can be a little or a lot, depending on the type of sensory disability they have.

Although learning disability, physical disability and sensory disability are all different, there is some overlap. Some people with learning disabilities also have a physical disability, or they may also have poor eyesight or hearing.

Can you 'catch' a learning disability?

No. A learning disability is not an illness. It cannot be 'caught' like a cold or mumps, so it is not true to call people with a learning disability 'ill' or 'sick' – although they can sometimes get ill, of course, like anyone else.

How does a learning disability happen?

A learning disability is caused by damage to the brain, either before birth or in early childhood. As a result, the brain doesn't develop as fully as it should. Sometimes the damage is only slight, so the learning disability will be slight too. But sometimes the damage to the brain is more severe, and also causes a physical or sensory disability. Someone with severe physical and learning disabilities may need a lot of help with things like eating, dressing, washing and getting around.

How does the brain get damaged?

The brain controls all the 'messages' we need in order to grow and develop. The brain contains many millions of cells and nerves, which can get damaged under some circumstances.

If a baby gets an infection, such as meningitis, when it is very young then the brain can be injured as a result, and may cause a learning disability. If the mother gets an infection, such as rubella (German measles), while she is pregnant then this can sometimes harm the baby's brain and cause a learning disability. That's why all girls have a rubella vaccination when they are about 10 years old.

A difficult birth can also sometimes cause a learning disability because the baby's brain may not get the oxygen it needs.

If someone gets a very hard knock on their head (maybe from a car accident or a fall off a horse) this can sometimes cause permanent brain damage and that person may then have learning disability.

Another cause of learning disability is something different in the chromosomes or genes in the body's cells – the 'building blocks' which make up the human body. This is how Down's Syndrome is caused.

What is Down's Syndrome?

Down's Syndrome is the most common kind of learning disability. The name comes from the word 'syndrome', which means a collection of signs or characteristics, and Down, who was the doctor who first described the condition in 1866.

You will probably already know someone with Down's Syndrome, or have met people with Down's Syndrome. People with Down's Syndrome have some similar physical features, such as distinctive eyes and mouths. But it is wrong to say that all people with Down's Syndrome look the same. Someone with Down's Syndrome will resemble their parents and their brothers and sisters, as well as other people with Down's Syndrome.

For every 650 babies born, one will have Down's Syndrome. It is caused by an extra chromosome in the body's cells. There are millions of cells in the body and every cell contains a number of chromosomes, normally 46. These come from our mother and father and carry all the instructions that tell our body how to grow. All our characteristics, such as our height, skin colour, eye colour and body shape, come from these chromosomes. People with Down's Syndrome have an extra chromosome, which disrupts the body's development.

What happens when children with learning disabilities grow up?

That depends on the person. Some people with learning disabilities find ordinary jobs and live by themselves or with friends. They may get married, just like anyone else. But many people with learning disabilities stay at home with their families, even when they grow up, because of a shortage of suitable housing.

Some people find work in 'sheltered employment', including work in an ordinary office or factory with costs shared by government. Others may go to day centres where they learn new skills and meet other people. They may also go to a college for further education (where you may go when you leave school).

If someone has a more severe disability, they may need a lot of help with ordinary things like eating, washing and going to the toilet. Some people with a severe learning disability live in specially designed flats and houses, with people to help them. But most live at home, and rely on the support of parents and families.

© Mencap
January, 1998

More special needs pupils to join mainstream

By Liz Lightfoot, Education Correspondent

More children with disabilities or learning problems are to be taught in mainstream classrooms in the biggest shake-up of special needs education for 20 years.

David Blunkett, the Education Secretary, said the Government wanted to speed up the integration of children with special needs which had been the trend over recent years.

'There is a forgotten army of 1.5 million children with some degree of special needs, many of whom would be able to flourish perfectly independently if the support was provided at the right time and in the right way,' he said.

Mr Blunkett, who was himself educated in school for the blind, said special schools catering for children with more severe problems would continue as an option for parents.

However, he envisaged a system in which local authorities would have a duty to offer a place in mainstream schools to all children whose parents wished it. Special schools would be centres of expertise, usually taking the pupils for part, rather than the whole, of their education.

Speaking of his own struggle to catch up with his peers and take examinations at night school which were not offered to pupils at his residential school for the blind, he stressed his determination that others would not face the same difficulties. 'When I was at a special school I was separated out from society. Integration once I hit adult life was a necessity,' he told BBC television.

'Getting it right in earlier years would have helped me get it right more quickly once I left school.'

The number of special schools has fallen to less than 100,000 and the proposals are likely to lead to further closures.

Publishing his Green Paper, on meeting educational needs, Mr Blunkett said the Government intended to overhaul the bureaucratic and costly process of statementing, which gives children a legal right to support, but can take up to 18 months.

The Green Paper suggests that a new system of co-operation between parents, schools and local authorities, including giving families a 'named' person to support them, would reduce the need for statementing in many less severe cases.

A reduction in statementing was viewed with alarm, however, by the Independent Panel for Special Education Advice which said it would strip legal protection from children.

Kate Symmonds, spokesman for the Panel, said the Government was proposing to 'cap' the number of statements. 'What the ministers see as bureaucracy, I see as the force of law protecting vulnerable children. Without that protection, children are left at the discretion of education authorities,' she said.

Mencap said the proposed reduction in statements indicated 'a complete lack of understanding of this vulnerable and often ignored group' which would leave 80,000 children with no assurance of an appropriately funded education.

However, the charity welcomed the 'appropriate and considered' integration of children with learning disabilities.

Some parents fiercely defend their right to choose special schools, saying their children could feel failures in comparison with other pupils. Other parents have taken local authorities to tribunals when they have refused their children into local schools, usually on the grounds of lack of facilities.

Yesterday, the second largest teacher union, the National Association of Schoolmasters/Union of Women Teachers, renewed its pledge not to teach children with severe emotional and behavioural difficulties who disrupted the education of their peers and posed a danger.

Nigel de Gruchy, its general secretary, said some children could not be dealt with in mainstream classes. 'It is totally unreasonable to expect teachers to perform miracles and solve all our deep-seated social problems,' said.

Mr Blunkett stressed that the question of disruptive pupils would be addressed separately.

© Telegraph Group Limited
October, 1997

Love, life skills and learning

For students with disabilities, colleges can be threatening places. But they shouldn't be. Stephen Hoare on a specialist college that puts independence high on the curriculum

Melanie Pullin has special needs. Twenty years old, paralysed down her right side and confined to a wheelchair from a stroke suffered as a teenager, she is one of 145 handicapped students at Lord Mayor Treloar College in Alton, Hampshire.

One of a handful of national specialist colleges, Lord Mayor Treloar has seen its numbers climb by around 10 per cent since the Tomlinson Report recommended improving special needs provision in FE. Attached to Lord Mayor Treloar College is an 8-16 school which is on a separate site but under the management of the same trust. Together, school and college provide an all-through route into FE. Around one-third of the 150 or so Treloar pupils go on to the college each year and, of those leaving the college, the vast majority go on to some form of higher education.

Graham Jowett, principal of the college, believes mainstream colleges pay only lip service to meeting the needs of disabled students. Occupying complex buildings on a multiplicity of levels and on different sites, they tend to segregate the disabled. 'Colleges can be very turbulent and threatening places for students with a disability,' he says. But Treloar is a residential college, and a key part of the experience is living in small family units, where students are encouraged to develop social skills and independence.

Built on one level and with wide corridors designed with wheelchairs in mind, Treloar's spacious classrooms are well equipped for special needs. The staff-to-student ratio is high, and there are nursing staff, occupational therapists and physiotherapists on hand to minimise the

time pupils have to be withdrawn from lessons for treatment. The technical department can adapt equipment to individual needs – anything from laptop PCs that can be operated by head movements for a student with no arms, to a computer that responds to commands via a voice synthesiser.

It costs between £20-40,000 to provide a student place, depending on the disability and level of support needed

---

But for Mr Jowett, the key benefit for his students is being among people with similar disabilities. When Melanie arrived at the college three years ago she was so frustrated at her inability to communicate that she was kicking and biting staff. Following a GNVQ in art and design, she is just another student and is as confident and bright as anyone of her age. 'In school or college, disability is the big issue,' says Mr Jowett. 'But here it isn't. Students are free to learn about their

peer groups, to form relationships and to fall in and out of love.'

Mr Jowett makes the obvious point that just because someone's body is disabled it does not mean their brain is disabled too. The college takes in young people with the severest handicaps – such as muscular dystrophy, spina bifida and cerebral palsy – and sometimes young people severely injured in road accidents. But 70 per cent of Treloar's students do have some form of learning disability, such as spatial awareness, and perceptual and orientation difficulties which need to be recognised and addressed.

As an FE college taking students between the ages of 16 and 25, Lord Mayor Treloar offers a full range of vocational qualifications – GNVQs and NVQs – as well as A-levels. The nearby Alton College accepts the more able-bodied Treloar students under a long-standing partnership arrangement. And for vocational courses – mainly IT, business administration, and leisure and tourism – the college has built good links with local employers such as banks or council offices, who each year accept disabled students for work placement. Treloar also has its own enterprise company, set up to provide work experience.

This sort of provision does not come cheap. Even though the college manages to attract some private sponsorship for computer equipment, and the Treloar Trust subsidises running costs by 10 per cent, it costs between £20-40,000 to provide a student place, depending on the disability and level of support needed. The costs of residential and medical care come to just under half the college's £10 million annual budget.

Funding is a major bone of contention. And with local education authorities (LEAs) and the Further Education Funding Council (FEFC) under pressure to cap costs, special educational needs (SEN) funding is being put under increased scrutiny. Below the age of 16, Treloar school can meet the needs of virtually any special needs statement; but, with funding cutbacks, many LEAs are fighting tooth and nail to keep statemented pupils in mainstream schools, regardless of the interests of the individual child.

Post-16, the FEFC is more open and accountable. The vast majority of Treloar's students are on recognised accredited 'Schedule 2' courses, which carry automatic FEFC funding. Only a handful of overseas students, or individuals who have received settlements for injuries, pay to go private. If the local sector college cannot meet the needs of a severely handicapped student, then funding follows automatically.

The whole funding package depends on contributions from a range of funding agencies; besides the FEFC, the main contributors are the local health authorities or council social services departments.

Funding can raise issues that are sticky to resolve – such as whether a specially adapted computer is for educational needs, or whether part of the cost should come out of the social services budget. Helen Burton, Treloar's admissions officer, says: 'The FEFC is becoming a lot more picky now and is looking for social services and the local health authorities to shoulder their fair share of the costs. The whole thing is becoming more of a paper chase.'

The delays make planning for places a nightmare. And, as the different departments of local authorities drag their heels, there is a real chance that some grants won't be agreed in time for the college to offer a place. In desperation, some

LEAs – such as Lewisham, south London, and Bromley, in Kent – have taken the unusual step of booking places in advance and say that they will underwrite funding even if the package is not in place.

Melanie and her classmates are the lucky ones. While the funding bodies squabble, many students who would clearly benefit from a place are having to wait, and some are going to lose out. It is a classic case that, if money is invested wisely now, it will reduce what could become a deferred social cost. Without the education and the experience of coping for themselves that Treloar College offers, many disabled youngsters would drift into a life of dependency. As Mr Jowett says: 'Our students live in a community where we give them the ability to build their self-esteem. We are training them for work.'

Council defends decision to bar disabled girl from school

By Jojo Moyes

A county council which told the parents of a disabled child that their daughter would not be able to attend the same school as her friends yesterday defended its decision, but offered her a glimmer of hope.

The parents of three-year-old Zoe Palmer, who suffers from spinal muscular atrophy, were told by Suffolk County Council that she could not attend Thurston Primary School, along with her friends from playgroup, because it could not afford the necessary alterations.

Richard Robinson, the council's spokesman, said that Suffolk had a budget of £10,000 for special needs improvements to 135 schools, and could not afford to spend 70 per cent of that on the chair lift and ramps that the council said the school would need.

The decision was criticised by Zoe's parents, who said that they had already raised £4,500 for an electric chair, and that they should not have to raise more money to get her into her local school. 'All she wants to do is go to the same school as all her friends in the village,' Zoe's mother, Juliet, 27, said.

But yesterday Mr Robinson said that Thurston school itself could apply to the Government for access grants, and that if it could raise the money, the council would not object 'in principle'.

'We strive as much as we can to ensure that every parent gets their child to go to the school they want to,' he said. 'This girl has another 15 months, another financial year to go before she even has to go to school. It's still very early, there's a lot of mileage.'

But he warned that even if Zoe Palmer were able to go to Thurston Primary School, she would eventually be faced with the same problem.

'The primary school have said that whereas they would love to have the girl at their school, at age nine she would still have to break off from her friends to go to another school because Thurston's middle school has no access,' he said, adding that the alternative schools the council had suggested were nearby and had good wheelchair access.

Zoe Palmer's parents could not be reached for comment on Mr Robinson's remarks yesterday.

The child with general learning disability

Information from the Royal College of Psychiatrists

What is meant by learning disability?

'Learning disability' used to be known as mental handicap or mental retardation. If a child has a general learning disability this means that, compared to most people, it is more difficult for them to understand and learn. Such a child will develop more slowly than other children of the same age even during pre-school years. The degree of disability can vary greatly. It can be so severe that the child is unable to speak and, even as an adult, will need help with ordinary tasks such as feeding, dressing, or going to the toilet. On the other hand, the disability may be mild so that, in time, the children grow up to become independent. However, even when mildly affected, it will be harder for the child to work things out. This will make it more difficult to cope with the more complex side of life, like managing money.

The more severe the learning disability, the more likely it is that other forms of disability will also be present including epilepsy, autism and various physical disabilities. These also vary in severity and may be so mild that they are missed if not looked for. For example, physical disability may be so severe that the child has difficulty in walking or using their arms. On the other hand, it may be so mild that it just shows as clumsiness in a child who has difficulty in learning to climb or run. Other disabilities can also be present, affecting the hearing, sight or speech and making it harder for the child to cope.

General learning disability is different from specific learning difficulty, which means that the person finds one particular thing hard but manages well in everything else. For example, a child can have a specific learning difficulty in reading, writing or understanding what is said to them, but their overall ability is normal.

What causes general learning disability?

This condition can arise from a variety of causes. These include genetic factors, infection before birth, brain injury at birth, brain infections or damage after birth (for example, Down's syndrome, cerebral palsy, Fragile X syndrome). In nearly one-half of the children affected, the cause of the disability remains unknown, even after a paediatrician (perhaps with the help of a geneticist) has carried out a full range of tests.

The effects of learning disability

The child or young person who has a general learning disability is aware of what goes on around them, including upsets and difficulties.

Great Britain figures

English figures
Adults with severe learning disability:
160,000

Children with severe learning disability:
30,000

Number of adults in 'hospital':
less than 8,000

Welsh figures
Number of people with learning difficulties known to services
10,000

Northern Ireland figures
Number of people with learning difficulties known to services
8,000

Source: MENCAP

However, their ability to communicate may be very limited, and this can make it hard to express themselves. Speech problems can make it even harder to make others understand feelings and needs. They are often frustrated and distressed by their own limitations.

For parents, the knowledge that one's child has a general learning disability can be a cause of great distress. It may be hard for members of the family to understand the cause of the disability or its effects. There may be great uncertainty about the nature of the problems. It can be very hard to communicate with the learning disabled child, and to manage difficult behaviour.

Learning disability and mental health

A general learning disability is not the same as a mental illness. It is a life-long condition, unlike mental illness, from which people normally recover. However people with general learning disability are more likely to suffer from emotional and behaviour disorders which can cause a lot of family stress. Children who suffer from autism or epilepsy are particularly at risk. Some people with general learning disability also suffer from mental illness. The family doctor will be able to offer help and advice. They may however benefit from help from a child psychiatrist with a special interest in learning disability and/or neurological problems. In these circumstances, the child may benefit from help from a Child and Adolescent Mental Health Service where the team will include child psychiatrists, psychologists, social workers, psychotherapists, and specialist nurses. Your GP or another professional can refer you or your child.

© Royal College of Psychiatrists

A class of her own

Nadia has cerebral palsy. But should that exclude her from a mainstream education? Her parents think not, even if it means uprooting the rest of the family. Amelia Gentleman reports

Not many parents would give up their job, sell their home and move over a hundred miles from their close village community to an unfamiliar part of the country, simply to place one of their children in the school of their choice.

Katie and Andy Clarke say that they had no alternative. Desperate to get their disabled daughter into a mainstream school, they have been forced to make some huge sacrifices. Both are fervent believers in the principle of inclusive education for children with special educational needs. They spent two years searching their area and neighbouring regions for a school prepared to accommodate Nadia, six, who is deaf and has cerebral palsy, while simultaneously appealing against the local education authority's decision to despatch her to a special school. Now, the couple have opted for the last resort.

They are now preparing for the upheaval of moving their four children from Northumberland to Calderdale, where they have been offered places this September for Nadia and two siblings, Dean, seven and Nikki, four, in the local primary school.

Keen to ensure that other people do not have to fight the same battle, the whole family yesterday came to London to join a demonstration outside Downing Street, calling for educational inclusion to all disabled children.

A governmental review on special educational needs issued last October expressed a commitment to inclusion, in principle, but campaigners are frustrated at the slow pace of change and that parents are still having to fight to get their children accepted.

The last few months have been extremely disruptive to the whole Clarke family. Sean, Nikki and Reay, two, will have to leave their friends behind in Ovingham, the village where they have grown up. 'It's hard for them, but they understand why we're doing it. They're very supportive of their sister,' Katie Clarke says.

People used to accuse me of not having come to terms with having a disabled child, saying that was why I wanted to put Nadia in a normal school

And the struggle to have Nadia included in the mainstream has opened Katie Clarke's eyes to depths of prejudice she had no idea existed a few years ago. Her experiences echo research published yesterday by the Leonard Cheshire charity, which revealed that disabled people remain the victims of widespread discrimination. As she explains: 'To begin with I was angry, but now I'm just sad. I can't believe that people are so quick to discriminate against a little girl. I feel like we're bring exiled, pushed out from our community because of a lack of understanding about my daughter,' she says.

The family's problems began immediately after Nadia's first year at nursery. 'She was the first disabled child in her nursery and she had a fantastic year. The children loved her,' says Katie. 'But she had to stay there for a second year while I tried to find a school that would accept her. She was very aware that all her friends had gone on to the big class and she had stayed behind.'

The village school, which her brother attends, said they did not have the facilities to accept her. Other mainstream schools said she was either too disabled or too deaf and that to include her would prove 'detrimental to the other children's education'; a place in a special school, a 50-minute taxi ride away, was offered. The Clarkes reluctantly accepted it – depressed that such a young child was being forced into segregated existence after they had worked so hard to include her.

'At home, we treat Nadia the same as the other children and because we've given her the same experiences, emotionally she's just a little girl of six – she loves Barbie dolls, she adores her new baby cousin, she's into clothes and going out shopping. She's extremely gregarious, very confident and very sociable,' Clarke says.

Far from being teased or victimised by her peers, it was the adults who were suspicious both of Nadia and her parents' attempts to keep her in regular school. 'The majority of the parents felt threatened or worried by her disability. People used to accuse me of not having come to terms with having a disabled child, saying that was why I wanted to put Nadia in a normal school. It was as if I was the one with the problem – had a chip on my shoulder. One person even said that people would move their children to a private school if Nadia had joined their school. I felt rejection from the community and I felt rejection of my daughter, which is really hard.

'I always wished the parents would watch how well their children got on with her, then they'd realise there wasn't a problem. The kids are brilliant – Nadia brings out the best in them. By staying in the mainstream, she'll get a good education and the other children will gain much more awareness about life and other people. It can only be an advantage for other children to be educated alongside disabled people.'

This conviction fuelled Clarke's prolonged search to find a school that would accept her daughter. She learnt that Calderdale Education Authority was one of the few local authorities to sign up to Unesco's 1994 Salamanca Statement – accepting its principles of wholly inclusive schooling. The authority offered to help as soon as she contacted them.

Despite her disabilities, Nadia is good at communicating with other children, and Clarke is confident that she will cope in the new environment. More than anything else, she is relieved that her daughter will now be able to reclaim her place in the community. She points out that other children will not suffer from Nadia's presence and her additional demands, because she is to be given a permanent assistant to help her. And she dismisses outright the argument that special schools have facilities and expertise that other schools cannot provide.

'As far as I can see, there are no advantages to special schools – there's nothing special about them. It's just about taking disabled kids out of the community and putting them into a segregated setting. That doesn't help anyone feel good about disability. If children are set apart from the age of two and a half, it makes it very hard for them ever to return to the community.'

She accepts that things may get harder for Nadia, as she gets older, but she argues that it's vital for her to learn how to cope with problems for herself. 'Any child can get teased, a child can become a victim even if they just wear glasses; I want her to be strong enough to give as good as she gets if she is teased. It's going to be tough for her when she gets older, but she's got a good beginning because she feels so good about herself now.'

The Clarkes' struggle will be familiar to parents of disabled children throughout the country. Although the Department of Education has supported inclusion in principle for years, little has been

---

'As far as I can see, there are no advantages to special school – there's nothing special about them'

---

done to make it a requirement and local authorities have widely varying policies on the issue.

Micheline Mason of the Alliance for Inclusive Education, which organised yesterday's demonstration, explains: 'At the moment, the law says that local authorities only have a qualified duty to integrate. The qualifications are that the child's educational special needs should be met, that the education of other children shouldn't be disrupted and that there should be an efficient use of resources. What that has meant is that anybody who wants their child to go to a mainstream school has to fight for their right to go there.

'If they are governed by a local education authority that doesn't have a policy on inclusion they will lose their fight. It's almost impossible to win the argument because these qualifications are so open to interpretation.'

She believes the Government's green paper on special education needs, published last autumn, despite reaffirming a commitment to inclusion, will change little. The slow pace of change has been frustrating for everyone involved in the campaign.

'There's no real financial argument – all we are asking authorities to do is transfer their resources from special schools to mainstream. But this requires people to abandon deeply held prejudices, the belief that these sort of people do not belong in the mainstream and they must stay in special schools where there are experts to look after them.'

Mason, who is physically disabled herself, adds: 'I was in a special school and it didn't prepare me in any way for the real world. We're not saying that children don't need help and we admit that sometimes that help must be given outside of the classroom, but we do not believe in permanent exclusion.'

Katie Clarke concludes: 'It makes me sad that we've had to move to get what we want for Nadia. It isn't easy moving with four children; my husband had to find a new job and we had to find a new house. But we felt we didn't have a choice.

'Nadia deserves the same educational rights as every other child in the country – I want her to get the best education possible. Developing relationships and having friends is all part of education and to take that away from a child is criminal.'
© *The Guardian May, 1998*

Learning disability

Information from Mencap

'A number of my friends have family problems. I have two sons with severe learning disabilities who have given me new interests, new friends, new opportunities, and a great deal of happiness'

(Father)

Words and people

Real people never exactly fit our descriptions of them. The most we can hope for is a description that says something worth saying and doesn't do too much damage. The terms 'mental handicap' and 'mental retardation' are now thought by many to do too much damage; and the less harsh 'learning disability' or 'learning difficulty' are used instead. In the pre-school years, 'slow development' or 'developmental delay' are often used.

The new terms are fairly broad and vague – which is no bad thing if it makes people go on to talk about individuals. No two people with learning disabilities are exactly alike. Even people with Down's Syndrome, who tend to have some physical features in common, do not all look alike; and they vary enormously in their health, abilities, interests, and characters.

When someone is described as having a general developmental delay or a general learning disability (which is not the same as being poor at maths or music or some other area of learning), it means two things. First, their intelligence is towards the lower end of the intelligence scale on which we all fit somewhere. Second, their social skills (their ability to adapt to new situations) are not as good as those of other people.

Room for improvement

Having problems with learning, development, adapting to new situations, does not mean that people with learning disabilities can't learn,

mencap

develop and adapt. It simply means that they take longer and may not go so far.

But it is also true that many people with learning disability are very good at certain things, including being good at making friends. In a group of five young people with severe learning disabilities who share a community home, there are two guitar players, one drummer, one artist, three gymnasts, five dancers, five singers, one outstanding jigsaw puzzler, five swimmers, one gardener, and five very nice young people, with whom it is a pleasure to share the evening.

Causes

Some people are born with a learning disability, for example those with Down's Syndrome. Others become disabled through a disease such as meningitis, or as a result of an accident. It is natural to look for an explanation when a child is born with some differences or does not develop as expected. An explanation may give clues about helping, but an explanation is not always possible. (Most of the old myths have been, quite rightly, swept away; but we don't necessarily have scientific answers to replace them.)

Sometimes the cause lies in the make-up of the parents (their genes), and as more and more is being learnt about this, it is a good idea to check with the GP, and to ask for further expert genetic counselling if necessary. Sometimes the child has a metabolic disorder, which means for example that some foods need to

be avoided because the body can't handle them normally. Again, ask the doctor. It may be possible to reduce some of the problems.

While it is common even for doctors who themselves give birth to a child with disabilities to worry 'Did I do something wrong?', it is very rare indeed for a child's learning disability to be anyone's 'fault'.

'Smiling is about the only thing Wendy can do for herself, but her smile makes my day'

(Regular visitor)

The future

Attitudes to people with learning disabilities are improving (slowly!). Opportunities for them are increasing (also too slowly). Until the 1970s, children with severe learning disabilities were not allowed to go to school. Now every child goes to school; and many go to ordinary mainstream schools. Until the 1960s, the choice for adults, and for many children, was either long-stay hospital or family home. Now very few people go into hospital and stay there, and there are a number of options, and much more support for families.

Futures are individual things; and there are some children with very severe disabilities who will never have much independence. Some may not live very long. Even for them, a great deal of loving, living and happiness can be packed into a very special sort of life.

'I cried three times in my life – once when she was born, once when she left school, and once when she left home'

(A parent who is also a professional working with people with learning disabilities)

Most children with severe learning disabilities are going to need more support than their peers throughout their adult lives. However, the problem for their parents may be coming to terms with the range of choices that their sons and daughters with learning disabilities can and do make. (Choices which are usually no worse, and sometimes much 'wiser' than those made by their other sons and daughters as they grow up.)

There are adults with learning disabilities who would once have been labelled 'hospital cases' now in paid employment, happily married, living in their own home, with a key to their own front door. Like other married couples, they may be grateful for what Mum and Dad did for them, and pleased to have Mum and Dad still within reach. Single adults with learning disabilities, living with friends or on their own, are also living full and quite ordinary lives – with help if they need it, when they need it. Their personal voices are increasingly, and rightly, being listened to directly by those in positions of authority.

Some don'ts and dos

Here are some points you might find helpful to put to relatives, friends, and neighbours, when challenging some of the false ideas that attach themselves to learning disability.

- Don't confuse mental illness and learning disability – any of us may become mentally ill, and if we do we can often be made better. A learning disability is usually something that people are born with and live with – and often learn to cope with.

- Don't believe any statement that 'All people with learning disability are . . . ' The only certainty is that they are all different.

- Don't forget that people with learning disabilities are likely to be happy, sad, angry, or pleased; and to want friends, pleasures, choices – just like everyone else.

- Don't imagine that because some people have few or no words, they have no thoughts or feelings either. Those who know someone who is very severely disabled very well, can often understand what they are saying, even though they don't 'say' anything.

- Do remember that people with learning disabilities are fellow human beings, entitled to as much respect as anyone else.

- Do look at people's strengths and not just their weaknesses.

- Do look at being part of the local community as something we are all entitled to; not something we have to earn.

- Do ask 'Why?' if you never see anyone with a learning disability in the places you visit and the company you keep.

- Do remember that things once thought impossible for people with learning disabilities are now taken for granted.

© Mencap
January, 1998

Beyond our means

Lindy Hardcastle on the plight of parents struggling to fund disabled students

Every parent whose child achieves a place at university must feel proud: how much more justifiably pride is felt when the child is blind or wheelchair bound, or struggling against ME or mental illness? These students need and deserve extra help – physical and financial.

My own son has Asperger's Syndrome, a form of autism, which made university life away from home and surrounded by apparently hostile strangers an insupportable nightmare. His physical and mental health broke down dramatically. Fortunately our local university was able to offer him a place with considerable support from its welfare services. Leicester University looks after more than 200 students with special needs, providing counselling, supported accommodation, study support, non-medical helpers for those with sensory and mobility problems and special equipment according to need – Braille machines, computers etc.

These services are funded by disabled students' allowances. We contacted Skill, the National Bureau for Students with Disabilities, which provided us with all the information we needed. Brilliant, we thought, until we read the small print. All these allowances are means tested against parental income.

As usual, it is the middle-income families that are hardest hit. My husband is a teacher and I am a childminder. We have two other dependent children and a mortgage, all of which is taken into account when assessing our contribution. The disabled students' allowances are considered to be part of the maintenance grant.

Until relatively recently, making up the maintenance grant to the full amount would have used up all the parental contribution of a family in our income bracket. Now grant levels are so low, our assessed contribution is considerably more than the £1,400 for a student living at home.

Therefore, my son receives no maintenance grant and we have to pay the difference towards his special needs support.

I feel strongly that the disabled students' allowances should be paid in the same way as tuition fees, as of right to any student gaining a place on an approved university course. Equality of opportunity is meaningless as long as there is a tax on disability.

© The Guardian
June, 1997

Parents caring for severely disabled children

A national survey of over 1100 parents caring for severely disabled children published in 1995 found that:

- Almost all parents reported at least one problem with the services they used. The most frequently reported problems related to parents feeling isolated from practitioners.
- Problems such as feeling that professionals did not understand what it was like to care for a disabled child, having to fight for services, and delays in service provision were reported by half the sample.
- Almost one-third of parents felt poorly informed about services and around one in five did not know where to go for information about services.
- Almost half the parents said their relationship with professionals was negative and unsupportive.
- Parents caring for a child with high levels of special care needs were most likely to be dissatisfied with services. They felt under pressure from professionals to carry out treatments and therapies.
- Over two-thirds of parents said they did not have a break from looking after their child as often as they needed. Despite this high level of need, three out of four parents did not use short-term care. One in three said they did not know such services existed and a similar proportion had chosen not to use short-term care.
- Family link schemes were the most satisfactory short-term care arrangements. However, most parents felt there were insufficient levels of provision of short-term care.
- Current levels of service provision, as well as types of services being offered, do not adequately meet the needs of disabled

children and their parents. This shortfall is exacerbated in black families, as well as those caring for children with the greatest care needs and social or behavioural problems.

- Almost 80 per cent of the children had at least one unmet need, and half had over four unmet needs. Areas of considerable unmet need include skills for future independence, help with learning, communication and physical abilities and treatments to improve the child's condition. Over a third of parents felt their child required help developing social or relationship skills, and a similar proportion said their child needed someone to talk to about being disabled.

- Among the parents, extremely high levels of unmet need were found in relation to having enough money to care for the child, help during school holidays and planning the child's future. The need for information about services remained largely unmet, as was the need to spend more time with one's partner and for help with the child's sleep problems.
- There was a consistent pattern of higher levels of unmet need among black families compared with white families.
- There are a number of groups particularly vulnerable to extremely high levels of unmet need and very poor living circumstances. These include parents from minority ethnic groups, parents on very low incomes, lone parents and those caring for children with extremely severe levels of impairment.

(Source: *Expert Opinions*, B Beresford, 1995, JRF)

© *NCH Factfile*

ADDITIONAL RESOURCES

You might like to contact the following organisations for further information. Due to the increasing cost of postage, many organisations cannot respond to enquiries unless they receive a stamped, addressed envelope.

Department of Social Security Information Division
Richmond House
79 Whitehall
London, SW1A 2NS
Tel: 0171 238 0781
Produces a range of leaflets on disability issues.

Disability Manifesto Working Group
12 City Forum
250 City Road
London, EC1V 8AF
Tel: 0171 250 3222
A national organisation working with and for physically disabled people. Ask for their publications list.

Disabled Living Foundation
380-384 Harrow Road
London, W9 2HU
Tel: 0171 289 6111
Fax: 0171 266 2922
Gives advice and information on any aspect of ordinary life presenting problems and difficulties to people of all ages with any disability.

Disablement Income Group (DIG)
Unit 5
Archway Business Centre
19-23 Wedmore Street
London, N19 4RZ
Tel: 0171 263 3981
Advises on benefits to which people with learning difficulties and their families are entitled. They also act as a pressure group for disabled adults.

Leonard Cheshire Foundation
Leonard Cheshire House
26-29 Maunsel Street
London, SW1P 2QN
Tel: 0171 802 8200
Fax: 0171 802 8250
Provides a range of care services for people with physical or learning disabilities and those with mental health problems. Produces publications.

MENCAP
123 Golden Lane
London, EC1Y 0RT
Tel: 0171 454 0454
Mencap is the largest charity in Britain working on behalf of people with learning disabilities and their families. Produces publications.

MIND
Granta House, 15-19 Broadway
Stratford
London, E15 4BQ
Tel: 0181 519 2122
Fax: 0181 522 1725
Mind produce a wide range of advice leaflets (45p each), reports and books. Has recently published *How to recognise the early signs of mental distress*, price £1 from Mind Publications. Ask for their publications list. Also produce the magazine *Open Mind*.

Mobility Information Service
National Mobility Centre
2a Atcham Estate
Shrewsbury, SY4 4UG
Tel: 01743 761889
Fax: 01743 761149
Provides information on all aspects of disablement mobility.

NCH Action for Children
85 Highbury Park
London, N5 1UD
Tel: 0171 226 2033
NCH Action for Children is the largest child care charity in Britain, offering a wide range of services and publications.

Opportunities for People with Disabilities
1 Bank Buildings
Princes Street
London, EC2R 8EU
Tel: 0171 726 4961
An employers' organisation concerned with recruitment, rehabilitation or career development of employees with disabilities.

Royal Association for Disability and Rehabilitation (RADAR)
12 City Forum
250 City Road
London, EC1V 8AF
Tel: 0171 250 3222
A national organisation working with and for physically disabled people. Ask for the publications list.

SCOPE
6 Market Road
London, N7 9PW
Tel: 0171 636 5020
Works to minimise the incidence of cerebral palsy during or after birth; works to enable people with cerebral palsy to achieve maximum independence and personal fulfilment. Ask for their publications list.

The Employers' Forum on Disability
Nutmeg House
60 Gainsford Street
London, SE1 2NY
Tel: 0171 403 3020
Fax: 0171 403 0404
Aims to promote employment for disabled people by making it easier for employers to recruit, retain and develop disabled employees.

United Response
113-123 Upper Richmond Road
London, SW15 2TL
Tel: 0181 780 9686
A national organisation which aims to create opportunities for adults with learning disabilities or mental health problems and support them to lead full and varied lives in the community.

Young Minds
102-108 Clerkenwell Road
London, EC1M 5SA
Tel: 0171 336 8445
The national association for children's mental health. Produces a range of leaflets, reports, a magazine and newsletters.

INDEX

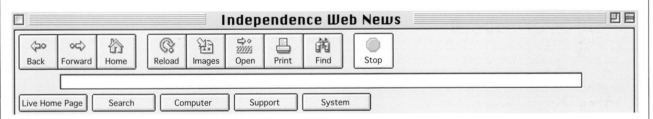

The Internet has been likened to shopping in a supermarket without aisles. The press of a button on a Web browser can bring up thousands of sites but working your way through them to find what you want can involve long and frustrating on-line searches. And unfortunately many sites contain inaccurate, misleading or heavily biased information. Our researchers have therefore undertaken an extensive analysis to bring you a selection of quality Web site addresses. If our readers feel that this new innovation in the series is useful, we plan to provide a more extensive Web site section in each new book in the *Issues* series.

* * * * *

Contact a Family
www.cafamily.org.uk
Contact a Family produces a wide range of factsheets, booklets and reports for parents, groups and professional workers. The text of all their factsheets (including one on caring for children with disabilities) is available free of charge on their web site.

Co-ordinated Campaign for Learning Disabilities
www.ldonline.org/index.html
A vast range of learning disabilities news and advice. US-based information but still quite relevant.

Disability Net
www.disabilitynet.co.uk/info/index.shtml
Offers a wide range of useful advice on a number of aspects of living with disabilities, press releases and links to other relevant sites.

Disability NOW
www.disabilitynow.org.uk/links.htm
Click on DN's list of useful web site links and you gets dozens of UK web sites covering most areas of disabilities.

Disabled People's Direct Action Network (DAN)
www.disabilitynet.co.uk/groups/dan
Lots of press releases and reports from this very active group.

Gateshead
www.disabilitygateshead.org.uk/rough/rough.htm
The Rough Guide to Independent Living was written by disabled people active in a number of disabled people's organisations. Offers useful advice on a number of aspects of living with disabilities.

Joseph Rowntree Foundation (JRF)
www.jrf.org.uk
The Joseph Rowntree Foundation web site contains several hundred research summaries (*Findings*) which can be accessed by keyword. Press releases and publications can also be accessed by clicking on the relevant icon in the navigation panel.

* * * * * *

ACKNOWLEDGEMENTS

The publisher is grateful for permission to reproduce the following material.

While every care has been taken to trace and acknowledge copyright, the publisher tenders its apology for any accidental infringement or where copyright has proved untraceable. The publisher would be pleased to come to a suitable arrangement in any such case with the rightful owner.

Chapter One: Living With Disabilities

Prejudice is the worst handicap, © The Independent, May 1998, *Disability daily*, © Disability Daily, January 1998, *Take up thy bed and work*, © Telegraph Group Limited, London 1997, *Harriet Harman's little problem*, © Social Security Statistics, 1997, *Benefits fraud by the disabled reaches £500m*, © Telegraph Group Limited, London 1998, *How the cuts would disable us*, © The Guardian, December 1997, *Totting up bill for illness and disability*, © The Independent, December 1997, *£10m disabled benefit 'goes to the better-off'*, © The Daily Mail, December 1997, *Are you disabled?*, © Department of Social Security, *Estimates of the prevalence of disability*, © Martin and others (1996) for 1985; FRS Follow-up survey of Disability for 1996/97, *Disabled demand end to 'apartheid'*, © The Independent, May 1998, *If you think disabled people get a raw deal*, © The Disablement Income Group (DIG), *Should disability benefit be cut?*, © The Daily Mail, December 1997, *Cash-in-hand scheme set to stall in the blocks*, © The Guardian, March 1997, *Industrial injury*, © Social Security Statistics, 1997, *Blighted lives*, © The Guardian, April 1998, *Hello, sister! Hello, brother!*, © NCH Action for Children, *Prevalence of disability among children*, © Health Survey for England 1995, SCPR on behalf of the DoH, 1997, *Unequal opportunities*, © NCH Action for Children, *No way out*, © Time Out, December 1997, *Fight on the home front*, © The Guardian, December 1997, *Disabled groups protest at 'inadequate' legislation*, © The Guardian, December 1996, *The man who would kill disabled babies*, © The Independent, May 1998, *Forgotten citizens*, © Disability Manifesto Group, *Children with a disability*, © NCH Action for Children, *Disability*, © The Industrial Society, January 1998, *Study shows disabled prejudice*, © The Guardian, June 1998.

Chapter Two: Disabilities and Learning

What is a learning disability?, © Mencap, January 1998, *More special needs pupils to join mainstream*, © Telegraph Group Limited, October 1997, *Love, life skills and learning*, © The Guardian, June 1997, *Council defends decision to bar disabled girl from school*, © The Independent, June 1997, *The child with general learning disability*, © Royal College of Psychiatrists, *Great Britain figures*, © MENCAP, *A class of her own*, © The Guardian, May 1998, *Learning disability*, © MENCAP, January 1998, *Beyond our means*, © The Guardian, June 1997, *Parents caring for severely disabled children*, © NCH Action for Children.

Photographs and illustrations:

Pages 1, 6, 17, 18, 20, 25, 32: The Attic Publishing Co., pages 12, 22, 29, 37: Ken Pyne.

Thank you

Darin Jewell for assisting in the editorial research for this publication.

Craig Donnellan
Cambridge
September, 1998